The Courage
to Be Real

*Becoming a Woman of
Confidence and Integrity*

MIRIAM BUTLER CONRAD

VINE
BOOKS

SERVANT PUBLICATIONS
ANN ARBOR, MICHIGAN

Vine Books is an imprint of Servant Publications especially designed to serve evangelical Christians.

Published by Servant Publications
P.O. Box 8617
Ann Arbor, Michigan 48107

Cover design: Hile Illustration and Design
Cover photograph: © Photodisc. Used by permission

99 00 01 02 10 9 8 7 6 5 4 3 2 1

Printed in the United States of America
ISBN 1-56955-102-2

LIBRARY OF CONGRESS CATALOGING-IN-PUBLICATION DATA

Conrad, Mariam Butler.
The courage to be real / Miriam Butler Conrad.
    p.   cm.   — (Women of confidence series)
ISBN 1-56955-102-2 (alk. paper)
1. Christian women—Religious life.   2. Christian women—Conduct of life.
I. Title.   II. Series.
BV4527.C645   1999
248.8'43—dc21   99-39991
                                                        CIP

Dedication

ℰᴧ

For Pastor Jimmy and Carmella Johnson
God's definition of *Real* People

Contents

Foreword

What hit me immediately about Miriam's book is its hospitable environment. I think you too will find yourself feeling right at home. I enjoy a visit with someone who not only welcomes me in, but gives a complete tour, allowing me to peek into the nooks and crannies. Miriam surely does that as she opens her life, her foibles, her fears, and her heart to our scrutiny. What I love most is that she does it not that we might know Miriam better, but that we might know Christ better.

To 'fess up to the Lord our secret sins is one thing, but to shout it from the rooftop to the rest of the neighborhood is downright threatening ... unless, like Miriam, you have stepped through to resolve. Once that happens it is difficult not to tell others in hopes that they too might know the freedom of forgiveness and the liberty of walking in the light.

This book is riddled with humor, which I found to be delightful, mixed as it is with Miriam's hard-earned insights. I was alternately tickled and touched by her struggles to come clean. I, Patsy, also affectionately known to the Lord as "Pig Pen," know how difficult it is to take the first step out of the pen and head for "home." The good news Miriam and I have found is that the Father waits with open arms.

I believe you will discover, as I did, that by the time you finish the book you will have begun a friendship with this courageous woman who gave up her carefully-constructed, well-ordered, properly-labeled, designer life to begin the risky undertaking of living honestly before God and others. And perhaps we too will throw caution to the wind and become illuminating examples to a world that's hiding in the shabby shadows.

Patsy Clairmont

Acknowledgments

ß∂

It could be said that writing the book was an easy task compared to preparing this page for publication. Like most first-time authors, I felt I had best do it right this time, or I might not get a second chance! So, with a grateful heart, I give thanks to God for the following:

Traci Mullins, my editor, who led me from tape to type with the gentlest of hands, a servant's heart, and a brilliant mind.

Gwen Ellis, who took the chance, and the time, to bring me to Servant Publications.

Kathryn Deering, Senior Editor at Servant, who has become not only a partner in publishing, but a sister in soul.

Dr. Judith Knox Corbin (alias BF), the Wind Beneath My Wings.

My husband Roy and our sons, Alan, David, and Christopher, for their help and encouragement.

Above all else, God Himself.

ONE

છે

The Agony of Deceit

You wouldn't have picked me as a likely candidate for a life of duplicity. I had been born in a pastor's home, given my life to Jesus at an early age, and been privileged to hold leadership positions in the church all my adult life. My public world was the picture of devotion to God. Many in the church where I served on staff considered me a role model for women in ministry. My husband and I owned a lovely home, which I kept clean enough to prevent serious disease. Together we had produced three reasonably well-disciplined sons who were in church willingly every Sunday. We looked like the poster family for Growing Up Born Again!

Things were not, however, as they appeared. I suppose I could say that there was a dark side to my personality. But as I recall, the truth would more closely be told if I said my life was primarily dark sides, with a little artificial light turned on when necessary. I had allowed sin, in many forms, to corrupt my mind, harden my heart, radically affect my choices, and distance me from God.

Sin is so deceitful. It had not swept down upon me like a sudden thunderstorm, blocking out the sun (or should I say Son?). Rather, it had come in droplets of compromise, of rationalization, of pride, of anger against many past injustices, and in heavy mists of insecurity and misconceptions about the character of God. Sin, once begun as a pattern of thinking and behavior, had infiltrated every area of my life.

Finally, on a May evening in 1977, I could no longer bear the agony of my own deceit. I'd already put my family through some hellish days as my life began to crumble under the weight of years of sinful behavior, yet there was still more to confess. Panic filled every pore of my body and spilled out through my quavering voice. "We have to talk after dinner, Roy."

That statement, which opened the way to the first real peace I had known in many years, shattered his quiet world … again. As he put down his fork, my husband's eyes reflected the weary but unspoken question of his heart: "What more could possibly be wrong?" Roy was exhausted. Physically, emotionally, and spiritually. Through three recent suicide attempts he had stood by me. I had leaned on him for support as I cried bitter, bitter tears. He had been as compassionate as he knew how to be as he listened to my confession of guilt regarding serious, damaging sin.

The garbage we had been sifting through together was messy and difficult. Through the gentle, incessant work of

God's Holy Spirit in my soul, I had somehow found the courage to make the toughest decision of my life: I would recommit myself to Roy and the sanctity of our marriage for as long as God kept us both on earth. The illicit relationship that had been consuming my thoughts, driving my actions, and had come very close to ending our marriage (and my life) would cease forever. With the prayerful support of some close friends I had been able to tell Roy everything concerning what had happened. He believed the worst was over. Now we were both working to restore a sense of normalcy in our home. Yet, as appalling and devastating as my story had been up to that point, there was more....

Someone once said that all of us have an inherent right to make any choice we desire. What we don't own is the right to pick the consequences of those choices. It certainly wasn't as if I didn't know that someday there would be consequences to this particular wrong choice I was now facing. Perhaps because the gratification was instant and the consequences were delayed, I found it easy to close my eyes to the pile of consequences as it grew in the third drawer of my bedroom dresser.

Bills from every department store in town, most of them with "past due" stamped in red, were hidden under my socks and slips. Those bills represented the magnificent wardrobe that hung in virtually every closet in the house—clothing purchased with credit cards bearing Roy's name. Roy, however, had not signed for those clothes and was not morally responsible for the bills, for he knew nothing about them.

You may wonder how Roy could be so clueless about all the

clothes and bills. The reason is simple: my husband is one of the most focused men you could ever meet. He sees only what is directly in front of him, especially if his mind is on other things. Roy does not notice even a new dress when I wear it (if it were a tool or a new part for his car engine, he'd see it immediately!), and once the first bills began to arrive, I made sure he never picked up the mail. That was one of my carefully planned schemes.

Early in the day I had begun the process of facing the problem. After the boys left for school, I dug out every bill from the drawer. I located a big, yellow legal pad and listed each store and the amount we owed. Then I searched through every purse I owned in order to locate all the credit cards I had hidden. I prayed that God would help me to remember every single bill.

I quickly became amazed at the magnitude of the problem I had created. My fear and apprehension grew alongside the list of debt and the pile of plastic. Debt—credit card debt in particular—is something in which Roy does not believe. Wait, that's not a strong enough statement. Not only does he not believe in unnecessary credit cards, he abhors them! He won't tolerate them! Debt is such an issue to him that he practically had apoplexy before he signed our first mortgage papers. Roy is so serious about this debt issue that he is convinced when we all get to heaven, God will judge sin in this order:

1. DEBT
2. MURDER
3. ADULTERY
4. ALL OTHER SIN.

That probably isn't how it's going to be, but the above list does clearly illustrate how Roy would judge the sins of the world, given the opportunity. It was his near obsession with living debt-free that fueled the terror in my soul.

With all that I had attempted to make right between Roy, myself, and God, somehow I had never worked up the courage to discuss the credit cards with my husband. Although a few weeks had passed since the worst of the crisis, the rest I was experiencing was sporadic and my heart was often troubled. There certainly was no peace in my soul.

What causes a person to finally give in and choose to do the right thing? In my case, I truly believe God was finally fed up with my sin and, because He loved me, He could not allow my life to continue on as it was. Jesus Christ had paid the ultimate price so that I could live a life free of sin, free of guilt, free of condemnation, free of hiding and duplicity. For the sake of His name—and for the sake of my soul—my life would have to change. This day, when I woke up, the burden of deceit and guilt was too heavy to bear for even twenty-four more hours. I would have to tell Roy what I had already confessed to God: I had spent money we didn't have. We were in trouble financially.

The evening meal was over. I quietly told our three young sons to go outside and play. They were to stay outside, I instructed, until I called them back into the house … or they heard a scream—whichever came first! I truly believed that the truth I planned to reveal in the next few minutes might be sufficient to cause Roy to react for the first time with physical violence. Everybody has a limit, and I knew my husband was right up against his.

Roy slowly pushed his chair back and said to me, "Let's go into the bedroom and talk there." The moment I had dreaded was finally here.

Roy sat down on the edge of the bed and I began to pace the floor. After a minute of strained silence, I handed him the yellow legal pad and the fistful of credit cards and said, "Look at what I've done. This is not your fault. It is mine. But Roy, I am truly sorry. And I am sorry enough to never do this again."

Roy took the list from me and looked at it for what seemed like an eternity. Sorrow, disbelief, disappointment, and confusion were written in every weathered line of his face. There was no way I could have prepared myself for his reaction. "Miriam, come here and let me hold you. Obviously you have needs I don't know anything about. If you will let me hold you, we will work this out together."

I will never forget the overwhelming relief that flooded my soul as he held out those big old farmboy arms to me and we embraced one more time. I was experiencing for the first time a human illustration of God's unconditional love. Love that doesn't keep an account of wrongs. Love that doesn't say,

"You've just gone too far this time." I now knew what God's perspective was on repentant sinners who come to Him with their "list."

The God of Compassion

We have all had them, you know, at one time or another, perhaps still today: Lists of current or long-ago issues that continue to separate us from a clear, pure relationship with God. Lists that reflect our own wrong choices, not the demands of an unreasonable God. Lists that are hidden under the socks and slips of quiet rebellion or insidious shame and the terror of coming out into the light.

God cannot allow us to keep on living this way. After all, He Himself is Light. Jesus Christ, the most real, transparent person who ever walked this earth, said of His Father: "God is light, pure light; there's not a trace of darkness in him" (1 Jn 1:5, THE MESSAGE). As God invades our lives, not only is He revealed by His Light, but we are illuminated also. Both our greatness and our nothingness, our holiness and our sinfulness, are exposed. We may be quite successful at hiding from everyone else, even from ourselves, but there is truly no hiding from God. "Great are your purposes and mighty are your deeds. Your eyes are open to all the ways of men; you reward everyone according to his conduct and as his deeds deserve" (Jer 32:19).

That truth used to fill me with fear and shame. Who knows,

maybe I'd already gone beyond some invisible boundary. Perhaps if I did admit my sin and come clean with God, He would lay some inconceivable discipline on me. After all, if the punishment is to fit the crime, I'm smart enough to realize I'm in big trouble.

Fortunately for all of us, constant misery brought on by severe punishment is not God's goal for me, nor is it for you. Harsh discipline is never God's first choice when dealing with us. He would much rather we respond to His initial acts of love and kindness. "I have loved you with an everlasting love; I have drawn you with loving-kindness" (Jer 31:3). What God really wants is to enter into a relationship with each of us that is built upon love, trust, openness, and intimacy. He has chosen to know us intimately not only so He can expose our sin and folly, but also so He can reward us for who we are and what we do that is pleasing to Him.

If you are like I was for so many years, you may be feeling like all these soothing truths apply to everyone but you. If anyone really knew all the ways you've displeased God, they would conclude that God's grace just doesn't extend that far! But reading the Gospels proves to us that Jesus understands our human condition completely, and feels with us when we are angry or lonely, frustrated or guilt-ridden, grateful or joyous. The apostle Paul counseled us, "Now that we know what we have—Jesus, this great High Priest with ready access to God—let's not let it slip through our fingers. We don't have a priest who is out of touch with our reality. He's been through weakness and testing, experienced it all—all but the sin. So let's walk right up to him and get what he is so ready to give. Take the mercy, accept the help" (Heb 4:14-16, THE MESSAGE).

Jesus' public ministry confirms that He really does know what is making your heart hurt right now. Remember the story of the brokenhearted former hooker who wept at his feet? In chapter 7 Luke tells us of this woman who had "lived a sinful life." Through the gossip grapevine, she discovers that Jesus is having dinner over at Simon the Pharisee's house that night. Motivated by gratitude and love, she decides to crash the party in order to get close enough to Jesus to carry out her plan.

As Jesus sits eating with the self-righteous host and his guests, the "woman of ill-repute" positions herself under the table at His feet. Being this close to the Savior who has forgiven her sin and given her hope for a radical change of lifestyle is overwhelming for her. Weeping, she begins to wash Jesus' feet with her tears, drying them with her long, beautiful hair. As the ultimate sign of sacrificial love, she pours expensive perfume on His feet.

When Simon sees this display, he thinks to himself, "If this man were a prophet, he would know who is touching him and what kind of woman she is—that she is a sinner" (Lk 7:39). Reading Simon's mind, Jesus comes to the woman's defense with a powerful condemnation of pharisaical self-righteousness. Jesus did not forgive and bless the woman because she was perfect ... nor because she had served Him in the past ... nor because she was deserving of His compassion and forgiveness now ... but because He knew the depth of her love for Him. He understood the powerful emotions that caused her to risk such an act of devotion, and His heart was tender beyond description as He watched her "work out her salvation" (see Phil 2:12).

Scripture is full of people just like you and me—people who are undeserving of God's gracious compassion but receive it anyway. Consider the adulterous woman in danger of being stoned, the deceitful Samaritan woman at the well, the disciple Peter who denied his Lord three times. Jesus had compassion for them all.

I once made a quick count of how many times I could find the phrase, "Jesus, having compassion ..." in the New Testament. With just a cursory look I located more than twelve passages. Then I tried to find a more specific definition of the word that is translated "compassion" in the Scriptures. What I found amazed me. First of all, there is no English word that can translate the full meaning of the Greek word *splanchnizomai* (splank-neets-zo-mi). We have had to settle for "compassion," or "felt pity for," or "had sorrow." But those words don't begin to describe the depth of emotions felt by Jesus for the ones who were hurting.

When the Gospels say Jesus was moved with compassion, they are saying that His heart was completely torn to pieces. This was far more than superficial pity on His part; His insides were ripped apart on behalf of the hurting one. The Greek verb attributed to Jesus is related to our word for "womb." The compassion of God for you and me is such a deep and powerful emotion that it can only be described as a movement from the very depths of His being. God's compassion for us is not based on our perfection, but on His character and determination to love us. One of my favorite hymns has always been "O Love That Wilt Not Let Me Go." The haunting beauty of the melody line, combined with the outrageous truth of the lyrics, deeply touches my heart each time I hear it. Only recently did I learn the story of how the song came to be written.

In the 1800s, in Scotland, George Matheson was born. Shortly after his birth the doctors discovered an eye defect which resulted in total blindness by the time George was eighteen. Almost immediately, his fiancée left him, making it clear she would not be content living out her life with a blind man. And so, in the midst of one of the darkest periods of his life, Matheson wrote:

> O love that wilt not let me go,
> I rest my weary soul in thee.
> I give thee back the life I owe
> That in thine ocean-depths its flow
> May richer, fuller be.

When we are brought face to face with our own imperfections, we need not hide, but are given the privilege of confidently bringing those very things that would defeat us to the feet of Jesus Christ. As we allow Him time and space to cleanse our hearts, infuse us with His strength and power, and change our perspective on perfection, we will learn to stand openly and freely in the circle of His grace.

No More Hiding

As I sit here writing today, I look into a set of mirrored closet doors. When asked to write on the subject of being real, I deliberately rearranged my desk so I would be forced to face myself every day. Sometimes I write late at night in my pajamas and with no makeup; other times I squeeze in a few minutes before leaving the house with makeup and hair in place. But no matter which it is, there is no way I can deny the reality of who I am.

I couldn't have done this a few years ago. I was concealed behind masks of pseudoconfidence, camouflaged with layers of frantic Christian activity, coated (I thought) by a strong veneer of competence in my career, and armored against any need or desire for intimate relationships. Many years before, when I was a child in tremendous emotional pain, a steel door had slammed shut somewhere in my throat, between my heart and my head. Because the door prevented my mind from registering the agony in my soul, I was far more willing to carry the load of pain, shame, and fear than to discard the door. Hiding in my head, far removed from the real feelings below, I could avoid coming to congruity about who I was, and I could deal with God and people on a strictly cognitive level, without risking any potentially painful invasion of the "real" me.

In many ways, this book is the story of the dissolution of the steel door. It is written with the fervent prayer that you will come to see the glorious blessings that result from coming out from behind whatever facades and fortresses you've created to protect yourself. Living a life of openness, integrity, and transparency offers rich rewards, which we'll examine in detail in the pages ahead.

But let me warn you right away, this lifestyle doesn't come cheap. In fact, you can't possibly afford it on your own. A real, courageous way of living comes at an exorbitant cost. How much? The lives of at least two people, one perfect, the other not even close to perfection. With His substitutionary death at Calvary, Jesus purchased for you and for me the privilege of living an open, confident, transparent life. As we choose to die to our own hiding mechanisms and replace them with the righteousness that is offered to us in Christ, we begin to emerge into the light of transparency and reality.

The ability to live an open life with ourselves, God, and others is possible only when His perfect love penetrates and insulates our hearts so that we can live with courageous transparency and conviction. If you've been a Christian for some time, that last sentence probably sounds like familiar religious lingo. You may have just scanned the words without letting the truth penetrate your mind. If so, read it again. And again. And again. Because everything else we're going to talk about depends on your understanding and personal experience of the unconditional love of God for you and your ability to develop confidence in exactly who He has created you to be—even when you're far from living out His perfect design.

True Reflections

1. You may never have lived a double life, as I did, but most of us hide our true selves to some degree. Take a few quiet moments and ask God to search your heart. Write down anything the Holy Spirit brings to mind about parts of yourself you tend to cover up or deny.

2. If you are convicted about a particular sin or sinful pattern in your life, try to be honest about the specific ways this behavior affects you and those around you. In what ways have you allowed sin in any form to
   - corrupt your mind,
   - harden your heart,
   - affect your choices, or
   - distance you from God?

3. Do you believe with all your heart (not just your head) that God is a God of compassion and mercy, and that any sin or burden you bring to Him will be cleansed and lifted by His grace? Why or why not?

4. Consider bringing your whole self—sins, secrets, strengths, hopes—into the circle of God's grace. Are you willing to expose all of who you are to Him and to the people closest to you? If not, ask yourself why.

ℰᴐ

Why Am I Afraid to Tell You Who I Am?

There is only one reason I'm willing to shell out the steep ticket price every year to get into the San Diego County Fair. Even with the senior citizen's discount (which I'm always offended they offer when I show up at the window), the outlay is no small matter to me. However, it's definitely worth the cost.

Once inside the gate I hurry past the pungent displays of pigs, goats, cattle, and chickens. I avoid the building where hawkers loudly ply their trade—selling all sorts of stuff I forget about in between July visits. Even the magnificent floral displays can wait until later. I am a woman of purpose, of destiny. I know exactly where I'm going.

When I finally reach the appropriate area, I willingly plunk down yet another hard-earned dollar to gain admittance to my destination, the infamous "Hall of Mirrors." After many consecutive years of faithful attendance, I have the maze memorized. Three more quick steps and I'm there, looking at myself as I've always dreamed I could be: 5'10" and skinny as a rail! For a few delicious moments I no longer struggle with the daily discipline of weight control and exercise. Who needs it? Forget the "ample petite" rack at the department store. Now I can double for some super-model! I've finally made it! Now I'm a real person! No longer do I have to explain that inside this size sixteen body is a size six woman, protecting herself with fat and cellulite for the promised glorified body at the rapture. I'm tall, slim, gorgeous, and ready to take on the world. I stand amazed!

And deceived.

A few minutes of wishful seeing come to an abrupt close as the line to get through the attraction piles up behind me. I move on, refusing to look at any other images of myself, vainly attempting to convince myself I really do look like that elongated, magnificent specimen of feminine humanity. Back out in the bright sunlight of the real world, I accidentally spot a reflection of myself in the mirror of the carousel. No amount of pretending can change reality: I'm still barely 5'4", and quite ample in form.

Don't get me wrong. I don't hate who I am. God gave me a particular body type, and I've come to terms with it. But sometimes it's just so delicious to pretend … to delude myself into thinking I'd be more lovable and acceptable if I were a transformed image of my physical self.

It's been a much more difficult, even sometimes torturous, path to come to terms with my true heart and soul. It was even harder to then fully reveal myself to God, and finally take the risk of opening myself to others. For most of my life I had looked for surroundings that would change who I really was into what I thought I should be. I built false environments that would keep me from having to face the truth about myself.

For example, I tried to surround myself with people I thought would make me "look good," regardless of whether these people whom I considered successful, gifted, and beautiful had character worth emulating. Far too often I found myself more absorbed with the appearance of the people I was with than with the state of their hearts. Somehow I believed that if I could run with those considered "winners" in my circles, I would become one of them. It troubled me not if these same folk were selfish, arrogant, and lacking in godliness or even the desire for holy living.

Residing in the "inner circle" shielded me from a couple of things. First, I was never faced with the poverty and need of those outside my little ghetto. I played with, attended church with, conversed with, socialized with, and sat in judgment with the "chosen few" (read "frozen"). Second, and far more seriously, spending all my time with those who lived and thought just like I did shielded me from the reality of what life "out there" is really like. If, by sheer accident, I found myself in a vulnerable position where someone might confront me with my arrogance or complacency regarding the needs of the world, I could quickly run back to the safety of "my own kind."

I may not have been clothing myself with fig leaves like Eve (it would have taken leaves enhanced by Miracle Gro!), but I was hiding in the garden of my own escape, just as she did. The problem, I eventually discovered, was that I couldn't hide forever. None of us can. Any temporary hide-out we may find only serves to further isolate us from ourselves, from the God we long to know intimately, and from any honest and meaningful experience of community.

Where Do You Reside?

This sin-cursed world is only too happy to provide for each of us unique fortresses behind which we can hide from others, from God, and even from ourselves. Hiding strategies and mechanisms are abundant. Let me list just a few—I'm sure you can add some of your own favorites!

The Burrow of Busyness

Whether we fill our days with a demanding career, homey crafts, delicious cooking, obsessive cleaning, or passionate religious work, these may all be equally effective in preventing us from coming face to face with ourselves.

When I was just past my seventeenth birthday, my husband, Roy, and I bought our first home. It was a fixer-upper (and I'm being generous), and for nine months we toiled to make it habitable. Roy would get up at 4:00 A.M., work on the house until 6:00, eat breakfast, and go off to his job at the telephone company. When he returned at 5:00, we would quickly wolf down some dinner and get back to the job at hand.

I worked harder physically than I had ever worked before. I was consumed with making decisions regarding such momentous issues as plumbing, nails, and how many cubic yards of concrete it would take for the foundation and the garage floor. For those nine months, Roy and I never took a day off, except for Sunday mornings. We didn't go out to eat, we didn't socialize with friends, we didn't see a movie, and we didn't take a vacation. We worked, period.

Perhaps it was good for me to work so hard. I certainly needed to learn the value and reward of hard labor. Yet I also mastered a dubious skill during that time, one that still tempts me today: hard work, especially when it leads to exhaustion, can prevent any extensive times of soul-searching, or renewal of soul.

This principle applies not only to physical labor, but to anything to which we give ourselves without taking time to step back and attend to whatever part of us is being neglected. Anyone can learn to hide behind too narrow a focus and too much exertion. It is easy to face the project but refuse to face the person. After all, if looking at all of yourself is too much, one can always remove the full-length mirrors in the house and replace them with those that show only the upper body. And if facing that much of yourself is still too painful, one can resort to a purse-size compact, or one of those tubular lipstick holders that will allow you to view only one-and-a-half inches of yourself. There are always ways to hide, if you look for them.

The Lair of Learning

Gwen was in her late fifties when I met her about twenty years ago. Tall, strikingly beautiful, with hair so white it formed a halo around her head, she seemed to exude holiness, confidence, and authority. When she came to our church as a recent widow, many of us younger women were drawn to her persona.

Word soon got around about Gwen's devotion to the Word of God and her commitment to long hours of study. Pretty soon several of us were making private appointments with her to seek out clues to her obvious devotion to the Lord.

However, just a few months passed before some of us were quietly conferring with one another regarding our disturbing impressions after meeting with Gwen one-on-one. Certainly her zeal for holiness was evident, her library extensive, and her time alone in study impressive, but this didn't stop her from making caustic comments about those who were "unwilling" to devote the same amount of time to devotional pursuits. From the pastor to the most stressed-out young mother, Gwen offered a uniformly critical assessment regarding their inadequate knowledge of Scripture and holy living.

Many of us proudly invest our energy in study. We are fascinated by the vast store of knowledge that is just beyond our grasp. We attend classes, write papers, take tests, participate in study groups, memorize Scripture, read voraciously, and wow people with our knowledge and brilliance. But are we investing the same kind of time and energy into building meaningful relationships with God and others? Is our study of the world's wisdom—or of God's—transforming us into people who love as He loves?

The Den of Denial

"Everything's great!" Anita would always say, smiling brightly. Nearly everyone who knew her, however, also knew that everything was not great. Living daily with an alcoholic husband and watching a daughter follow her footsteps into an abusive relationship wasn't "great." But as long as Anita could smile, she didn't have to cry. While keeping everyone at arm's length, her soul also lay buried beneath layers of denial. Not even God was allowed to visit.

Denial can be deadly. Literally. The inability or unwillingness to face reality and what is happening to us will ultimately result in disastrous consequences within us—physically as well as spiritually. From my own personal experience with denial, I can testify to the burning in my stomach, the headaches, and the overwhelming desire to sleep in order to forget. Much has been written recently about the physical manifestations of unresolved psychological and spiritual issues. Even medical science proclaims that the den of denial is hazardous to your health!

The Attic of Addiction

I used to believe that the only people who were addicts were the scruffy down-and-outers who willfully began a habit which eventually led to ruin. I no longer hold such a haughty judgment. Many, many temptations can quickly grab any one of us and cause us to flee from the "living room" of life to the attic, where we can hide safely with our "supply."

Someone you know well may be addicted to pornography. The excessive spending of money on anything can become addictive. Prescription and illegal drugs, alcohol, and gambling all provide effective fortresses behind which the enemy of our soul can keep us from living in reality and truth.

The Cave of Caretaking

Roy had just spent several months in the hospital, and then more time in a rehabilitation facility. During the crisis weeks God had graciously supplied others in our church congregation to "carry" me through their prayers and practical support. The real crisis was now behind us. Roy was home and quite independent, though still weak. He didn't need my constant care, and even was able to cook simple meals again, which he loves to do.

However, I hadn't shifted out of my caretaking mode. I had found some strange security in being solely in charge of everything, including him, and maintained my attitude of control and constant inquiry regarding how he was doing. Of course, while caught up in all of this, I had neither the time nor the desire to consider how *I* was doing. What had happened to my own heart during these months of confusion and near-death experiences? Had I taken any time to evaluate my own current relationship with God? Was I willing to face some of the anger and frustration I was feeling because of lack of sleep, too many trips to the pharmacy, and long, frightening nights in intensive-care waiting rooms? No, it was easier to determine to retain my "strength" so that I could continue as the ultimate caretaker. I didn't have the time or the energy to face my own needs, or my soul's brittleness.

Of course, I couldn't maintain such high levels of energy-sapping activity forever. Pretty soon God sent a visiting nurse, who told me to quit treating Roy as if he were about to die. "If you don't let him live a little, he won't," were her exact words.

I knew things had to change. Letting go of Roy and my need to control his every move was not easy for someone as stubborn and born to be in charge as I. But in the process of emerging from the cave of caretaking, I walked once more into the light of God's perfect plan for me, and for Roy, and into the reassurance that God alone is in charge of caring for those we love. I did not have to be Wonder Woman. I no longer needed to hide my real feelings and my human limitations behind the cape of a superhero—one who was actually full of fear.

Why We Hide

Why do we hide? In a word: fear. Being real and transparent just seems too scary. After all, if people *really* knew us …

Why do *you* hide parts of yourself or stay on the sidelines of the abundant life God wants for you as His beloved child? Again, let me suggest a few reasons, just to encourage your thinking.

Memories of Humiliation

I know I am running a risk when I confess this, for not many
women are willing to admit it: I love football! As August slips
into September, I look for every pre-season game on TV.
When Monday Night Football begins, I plan dinner menus
that can be easily eaten off a TV tray. My entire family has
memorized the theme song by Hank Williams Jr., "Are You
Ready for Some Football?" We sing along and scream our glad
"yesssssssss!" We are loud and opinionated fans, yelling for and
against coaches, players, and even some fans and cheerleaders.

The running back for our favored team always gets some of
our loudest cheers and groans. For those less familiar with the
game, let me explain in concise, simplistic terms the basic job
description of the the running back. He is the one who is supposed to take the ball from the quarterback and run down to
the goal line for a touchdown. The ball may have been
handed off to him, or thrown downfield, where the plan is for
him to catch it before either he or it hits the ground. Just like
life, however, the game does not always go according to plan,
and sometimes even the most experienced running back drops
the ball. This is not good. This is, in fact, sometimes very bad,
in that it results in what is technically termed a "fumble," at
which point the opposing team picks it up and may run for a
score of their own!

The game of football has no mercy, however. This same
fumbling running back is often required to carry the ball again
on the next play his team makes. No matter that he messed up
last time, looked like a dork, and may have cost the team the

game. The fact is, if he is ever to be an effective player again, he has to force himself to carry that ball one more time and prove that he's able to get it down the field.

You see, his failure is not final. But sometimes we think ours are. We may have messed up royally in the past and experienced haunting humiliation. So rather than face the jeering crowds and come back into the game of life, we run to the locker room, take off our uniforms, and refuse ever to play again.

Fear of Failure

When I left my job at Skyline Wesleyan Church in 1990, I was really excited about my new position at Point Loma Nazarene College. For the first time I had a title that had a little class to it: "Director of Special Projects." I remember so well taking a few days off between jobs and visiting Yosemite National Park with Roy. Every once in a while, I'd smile and say out loud, "Roy, I'm a Director!"

The glory quickly faded after the first five days on the job. Suddenly aware of the enormity of heading up the Conference Services Department, I began to panic. "It's no big deal," my boss assured me. "All you have to do is fill all one thousand dorm rooms with conferees each night during the summer, keep the rooms clean, keep the clients happy, feed everybody three times a day, assign meeting rooms, provide all media equipment, and accomplish this with a team of totally inexperienced student helpers. Not a problem."

For several days following that conversation I was virtually paralyzed in spirit. I had no concept of how to go about filling those rooms, or carrying out any of the other daunting tasks ahead. I very seriously considered immediate retirement, so nobody would have an opportunity to discover that I didn't know what I was doing.

Fortunately, my predecessor came back for a few days in order to provide some training. My confidence level began to rise just a teensy-tiny bit. I delayed resignation each week. Now I can say that the first summer may have been rough and tough, but it was very successful.

It would have been easier to quit. Quitting would have prevented me from ever having to face what was ahead. It would have removed my fear of an uncertain future, and the possibility of going down in flames. The future is always uncertain, and a less than sterling performance is sometimes gua nteed. Yet hiding behind the fear of "what if's" gives only temporary relief, never permanent peace.

Pride

Nearly twenty years ago I was heavily involved in an internationally-known Bible study program. My first responsibility was to be the pianist at the weekly gathering. Then I was "promoted" to leading a small group. Soon the number of women in the San Diego area who wished to attend outgrew the facility where we were meeting and it was determined that another study would be started in one of the outlying suburbs.

The woman who was leading the current group came to me privately and asked if I would be willing to spend the next few months training to become the leader of the new study. I was so flattered! For seven months I went through the interview process, spent many weeks in training, and submitted pages and pages of applications, statements of faith, and mock-ups of lessons and presentations. All the preparations for the new class were coming right along and I was flying high!

And then the sky fell. With only two days left before the new group was to meet, I was informed that I would not be leading the class. A woman with many years of experience with this particular group had been suddenly transferred to San Diego because of her husband's job. "Surely you understand that she should have first opportunity—for the sake of the women attending, of course."

No, actually I didn't understand. I was devastated, confused, and embarrassed. All my friends had sent me congratulations, had promised to pray, and some had even signed up for the class, just because I was going to teach it. What was most difficult was the rumor mill that went into full operation immediately: "There must be some other reason"; "How could she possibly have messed up so badly before she even started?"; or, most hurtful of all, "She wouldn't have been my first choice, anyway."

Crushed and humiliated, many months passed before I could return to any leadership position. I hid at home for weeks. Unable to face the questioning looks and unwilling to answer the same old questions, I found hiding in the comfort of my office and my home to be far superior to facing up to the wounding of my pride.

Shame

For several years I enjoyed mentoring small groups of women who felt called to public ministry. We called the group "Certain Women," and met once a month for fellowship and training. Most of the women in the group were recommended to me by members of the pastoral staff of our church. I specifically chose that manner of selection, believing that the pastors had some opportunity to see these women "in action," and already knew they had a heart for God and for ministry.

Merlina was one such young woman: smart, well-groomed, always punctual, absolutely dependable, and willing to serve. When one of our pastors suggested to her that she might be a candidate for Certain Women, she was uncharacteristically hesitant and insecure. However, she made an appointment with me and we had a short talk about the program. She agreed to participate in the next session.

The first assignment the women were given was to prepare a testimony for delivery in front of the rest of the group. Within a few hours of that first meeting, Merlina called. She asked if we could meet in a park not far from where she worked. She specifically mentioned that she wanted to talk where no one could hear our conversation.

We brought our sandwiches and sat at a table in the sunshine, but the bright light could not dispel the darkness that enveloped the lovely young lady. Long ago, as a child, she explained, she had been involved in ritualistic sexual abuse, against her will. Although she had gone through extensive Christian counseling as an adult and maintained a busy role in the church, Merlina was convinced she was "spoiled goods," could never marry, and certainly was ineligible for public ministry.

I wish I could tell you there is a happy ending to this story, but I cannot. The last I knew, Merlina had returned to her passive role in church activities, and refused any further personal healing or growth as a woman called by God to minister publicly to others.

When we are mistreated or abused, it can be a short journey to the pit of shame. Those of us who have been victimized by sexual abuse, domestic violence, or emotional or spiritual abuse are prone to feeling responsible for our own victimization. After all, we reason, we must be very bad people if others have seen fit to hurt us so. When we are convinced we're wrong all the time, and everybody else is right, the temptation to hide our "wrongness" is all-consuming. There is no way we are going to risk letting anyone see our emotional nakedness—not even God.

Guilt

When everything we value goes up in flames because of choices we have made, we can make one more bad decision to lie right down in the ash heap forever. We can wallow in our deep disappointment over our loss of reputation and resolve. We can walk around with our heads down and stare at the dirt for the rest of our lives. We can try to hide from God and from people. We don't have to, but we can.

Dan was a man of great vision and some planning, but

mediocre to terrible follow-through. At his urging, many of his friends invested in his dream to bring his latest invention to market. When everything fell apart, not only did Dan lose everything he owned, many of his friends lost substantial amounts of their savings as well.

Dan has never fully recovered financially. Neither has he chosen full spiritual or emotional recovery. For him, every day is another opportunity for shame and guilt. No matter how much those of us who love and respect him attempt to encourage Dan back into the mainstream of God's love, forgiveness, and blessing, Dan will not embrace restoration. For him, it is easier to stay mired in guilt than to face the future and start again.

Sometimes our guilt is the result of actions much more diabolical than Dan's. What may have begun as an "innocent" flirtation careens out of control and causes indescribable heartache to people who love us. What begins as "fudging" on our income tax becomes a refined skill of defrauding others. A "simple diversion" is how we may justify dabbling in pornography or gambling. Sharing the innermost terrors and regrets of our lives in a prayerful setting may trigger an unexpected "high" at knowing such private information about others. Soon the need to prolong the feeling drives us to share information that is not ours to share. Gossip may become our pet sin.

Even the most appalling sins need not condemn us to eternal exile from a life of love, abundance, and integrity, however. After we confess and turn from our destruction, using any past sin as an excuse for suppressing God's glory in our lives only compounds the sin. It is a serious matter to refuse to accept His forgiveness and love, turning our backs on His desire to provide unique opportunities to share that love and restoration with others. God never expects any of us to live in isolation because of past sin. If we choose to live out our lives in hiding, then we are simply demonstrating our profound unbelief in the grace of God.

Living Real

Most of us long for a life where all pretense is left behind and being real with each other is the norm. We don't want to have to worry about whether we will be misunderstood, mishandled, or misquoted. We want to be able to feel secure with those who surround us every day. As women, we long to be able to trust our casual friendships, as well as those with whom we are more intimate. We long for the guts—as well as the grace—to speak with firmness regarding issues that touch us deep in our souls. We need the confidence that is essential to facing the world without masks, without fear, without separation and alienation.

These are the struggles we're going to talk about in this book. We're going to discover that integrity is not an external façade, but the result of an internal focus. We'll talk about real people, real circumstances, real failures and victories, real growth and setbacks. We'll face the uncertainty of human relationships, the temptation to pretend, the difficulty of continuing to fight the good fight when others say the battle should have been won long ago. We'll face the heartbreak of being deceived by those we thought nearly perfect. Most of all, we'll look to Jesus, our perfect model of the courage to be real. "He had done no wrong, and he never deceived anyone" (Is 53:9, NLT).

Fortunately, Jesus is far more than a model. In many ways a model only illuminates how poorly we measure up. What we need is hope—deep confidence that change is possible. Jesus is that source of hope, a deep well from which we may drink confidence until we are saturated by its cool refreshment. Even more than this, Jesus *is* our confidence. He is open with us, He speaks truth to us. Rather than resenting our honesty, our questions, our doubts (even about Himself), He draws closer to us as we become more open, vulnerable, and real in our interactions with Him. He gently convicts us when we slip into falsehood. He urges us to come clean, to open our hearts to His love and cleansing. He listens with compassion to our confessions and persistently leads us into the rarefied atmosphere of transparency and light.

Living "real" is a process, not a destination. We can participate in the process every day of our lives. Each time we choose to be honest with ourselves about our questions, confusions, doubts, fears, and anger—as well as our unique joys, convictions, hopes, and passions—we are moving toward integrity. Each time we immediately bring those very same issues to God for His help, understanding, and affirmation, we become people living in the light. When the circumstances are right and we are called upon to be honest and authentic with people and we make the tough decision to live a transparent life (even when it scares us to death!), we are being transformed into women of God whose ultimate confidence comes from having nothing to hide—from God, from ourselves, or from each other.

If you're a young woman with most of your life ahead of you, the message of this book can revolutionize your experience and enjoyment of life. Jesus came to give us abundance, not some metaphysical, otherworldly, sad-sack, deprived, pickle-faced existence. Listen: "I came so they [you and I] can have real and eternal life, more and better life than they ever dreamed of!" (Jn 10:10, THE MESSAGE).

Or maybe you're a more mature, sophisticated sort, such as myself (well ...). Look here, I'll be sixty years old before you ever read this book. My metamorphosis from hidden to revealed didn't happen all at once, and much to my regret, it didn't even begin until just a few years ago. So if you think you're too old to change, wake up! As long as you can breathe and think, you can make decisions. And as long as you can make a conscious decision, you can change! As long as you are willing to change, God is willing (and quite *eager*, I might add), to help you along. I will hear no more of this "I've fallen down and I can't get up" mentality! So, old, young, or in between, today is the day to begin allowing God to make you into a "real" woman.

Now, don't despair if you don't know how to make this whole integrity thing happen. In the pages ahead you'll find plenty of ideas for incorporating transparent living into your daily existence. The questions and suggestions at the end of each chapter are designed to help you remember what you have just read and then apply it to your experiences.

May God become so real in our lives that any fears of "reality living" will be swallowed up in His glorious love and light.

True Reflections

1. I chose all-consuming work and the "inner circle" as false environments so I wouldn't have to face truth. Which of the common hiding places described in this chapter ring a bell of familiarity for you?

2. Have you been able to identify specific reasons why you are tempted to hide from yourself, from God, from others? Consider whether your reasons fall under one of these broad categories:
   • memories of humiliation
   • fear of failure
   • pride
   • shame
   • guilt
   What can you add to this list?

3. You might find it easier than I have to share your questions, confusion, doubt, fear, anger, conviction, hope, and passion with God. But if you need some encouragement, let me suggest a new habit you can begin creating today: each time you have a few quiet moments alone with God, determine to mention just one fear and one joy or victory when you talk to Him. Consciously bring these feelings and experiences "into the light." Notice your growing experience of the biblical truth: "But if we walk in the light, as he is in the light, we have fellowship with one another, and the blood of Jesus, his Son, purifies us from all sin" (1 Jn 1:7).

THREE

⁋

Just As I Am?

If you add two and two, what do you get? My guess is that without much perspiration or consternation, most of you came up with four. Right? That's because it is the nature of mathematics that the answer is four when you add two and two. And it is the nature of God to love you without condition.

It seems to me that many of us have got this whole spirituality thing backward. We think that the Christian experience consists primarily in what we do for God. We cheerfully and gratefully acknowledge Paul's words to the Ephesians: "For it is by grace you have been saved, through faith—and this not from yourselves, it is the gift of God—not by works, so that no one can boast" (Eph 2:8-9). But once that salvation transaction is complete, then everything changes, and instead of resting in what God has done and is doing in our lives to bring about our greatest good, we exhaust ourselves as we "work out our salvation," wrongly believing that now everything is up to us. But, to quote from Paul again, it just ain't so (well, maybe he didn't put it exactly like that ...):

> So, what do you think? With God on our side like this, how can we lose? If God didn't hesitate to put everything on the line for us, embracing our condition and exposing himself to the worst by sending his own Son, is there anything else he wouldn't gladly and freely do for us? And who would dare tangle with God by messing with one of God's chosen? Who would dare even to point a finger? The One who died for us—who was raised to life for us!—is in the presence of God at this very moment sticking up for us. Do you think anyone is going to be able to drive a wedge between us and Christ's love for us? There is no way! Not trouble, not hard times, not hatred, not hunger, not homelessness, not bullying threats, not backstabbing, not even the worst sins listed in Scripture ... none of this fazes us because Jesus loves us. I'm absolutely convinced that nothing—nothing living or dead, angelic or demonic, today or tomorrow, high or low, thinkable or unthinkable—absolutely *nothing* can get between us and God's love because of the way that Jesus our Master has embraced us.
>
> ROMANS 8:31-39, THE MESSAGE

If you're like me, you probably have trouble transferring these words from your head to your heart. You may have heard these Scriptures all your life, read them over and over again in your devotional times, and still not been able to wrap your heart around the liberating truths they proclaim. Comprehending and applying the full reality of a God who loves me unconditionally is a gigantic task. I, along with you, have had too much exposure to and experience with conditional love. It will require my entire lifetime to even begin to comprehend the way God loves me.

It has been my lifelong struggle to resist remaking God in my mother's image. She was judgmental, she loved to punish, and her driving motivation was to cause pain. God must be like her, I have reasoned. Better to avoid Him, better to hide than to face up to my own failures and disappointments. I have been so deceived as to believe that stopping long enough to be found by Him—out on the vast plain of my weary soul—would mean punishment, pain, and annihilation. I have mistakenly conjectured that God's ultimate motivation is to say "gotcha" and gleefully watch me squirm in my misery.

I'm still trying to come out of hiding completely. But in the process, I've learned a few things about His love.

God's Love Is Relationship-Based

I think every woman needs at least one "best friend"—someone with whom she can perform such essential tasks as trying on makeup, bathing suits, and blue jeans. Someone who will tell her the truth about her hairstyle, her choice of drapery fabric, and her latest culinary delight. Dr. Judith Knox Corbin is such a person. She is often brutally honest when I would at least temporarily prefer her to lie! She is quite frank with her comments when she feels I'm out of line with Roy or my kids. She hates pink (which is right near my favorite color), and she hates it when I wear it!

On the other hand, Judy is totally and fully committed to loving me in spite of my faults, failures, and foibles. She believes I am the most gifted, talented, and beautiful (for an old lady!) person she knows, and she tells people so. She believes in my unique calling, she encourages me to practice the piano, and she is patiently reading these chapters as I write them. This last favor is no small matter, since Judy has her doctorate in literature!

Most people who see Judy and me together believe we must have been friends all our lives. In fact, we've known each other fewer than ten years. Judy attended a seminar I presented, talked to me afterward, and invited me to have dinner with her the next week. Before dessert was served after that meal, a bond had been formed that still amazes both of us.

When Judy walked into my life, she immediately began to redefine my understanding of the word "friendship." With years of "measure-up-or-get-out" behind me, I'd only known one long, enduring relationship, and that was with my husband. Following the first serious quarrel Judy and I had, I realized there was nothing that held us together. No marital vows, no public pronouncement, no God-sealed commitment. I was fully aware that she was free to walk away from our relatively new friendship with no obligation to me whatsoever—especially since I was the idiot who had started the argument!

To my amazement, she didn't leave. Physically and emotionally she remained available and understanding. We talked through the matter of disagreement (would you believe it was on a point of theology?) until we could come to a mutual respect of each other's opinions.

Through the years, as the relationship has matured, we've continued to find both similarities and differences that make our friendship unique and vital. Just this past week we were shopping together (she hates it, I love it), and the clerk asked if we were sisters. "No, just best friends," we answered. Her reply was one we have heard countless times from store clerks, airline attendants, and casual observers: "Wow, I wish I had a friend like that."

What kind of a friend is Judy? She's committed to me, period. I have done some pretty stupid things since I met her (she's not perfect, either), and although she's perfectly honest about my stupidity, she never threatens to walk out or punish me by silence. She believes in me, trusts me, and confides in me. Not because she's obligated. Not because my friendship will somehow benefit her financially or professionally. She has made a choice: she will be my friend forever. Her friendship models God's relationship-based love to me.

What does it mean when I say that God's love is relationship-based? First let me tell you what it doesn't mean. It doesn't mean that He loves you in order that you'll experience love and, as a result, be a better mommy to your children—although once you truly know His love, you'll probably be a more loving parent. It doesn't mean that God loves you so you'll feel ashamed that you can't love Him back to the same degree, and therefore decide to give your life in some sort of service to try to prove how much you appreciate His love—although experiencing His love does create in most of us a longing to love and serve Him in return. Relationship-based love means just that: the reason you are loved by God today is simply because He flat-out wants an intimate relationship with you.

God's Love Is Grace-Based

It was the springtime of 1994. The college chapel service was packed to capacity. The speaker for the morning was Brennan Manning, a former Catholic priest, now well known through-out the world for his talent as an author and speaker. I took an aisle seat so I could slip out without much commotion if I got bored.

I was less than impressed by our visiting speaker when I saw him. The sleeves of his bright green cardigan sweater were far too long for his arms. His rapid-fire speech, seasoned with a strong New York accent, made him difficult to understand. I really had to pay attention to even decipher his words. But pay attention I did, for as Dr. Manning spoke, I began to sense that God was about to do something deep within my soul.

Then I heard it, the one sentence that would change my concept of the relationship between God and me forever: "God loves you, just as you are and not as you should be, for no one is as they should be."

Just as I am? Oh, could that be true? You mean I don't have to change in order to be loved and accepted by God? I don't have to clean up my act? He's not disappointed in me as I'm so often disappointed in myself? I don't have to somehow work my way back into His good graces? I believed that I might be acceptable to God in a "just as I am" state when I first came to know Him, when I was a spiritual infant; but now that I'd had some time to grow up, surely His expectations of me were far greater. The conditions for being accepted by Him must be more stringent. But suddenly, after being God's child for more than thirty years, Dr. Manning's simple words were pouring into my deceived heart like balm on an ancient wound. By now I was sobbing quietly into my hands.

That morning I finally "got it": You and I are to come to God in faith that He will keep His word and accept us "just as we are and not as we should be," and then permit Him to continually change us into His likeness. Of course God wants us to change. Of course God's best for us is that we forsake our sinful habits. Certainly it is God's desire that we come to love Him so completely that we choose to serve Him through our good works. But holiness is not a requirement for His compassion toward us. Being more righteous won't get God to love us more. "While we were still sinners, Christ died for us" (Rom 5:8).

Remember the exploits of God's chosen nation, Israel? The Old Testament tells us that the people's fickle hearts deliberately and repeatedly turned from following the God who loved them and promised them incredible blessings and protection, and instead they chose to live independently and to worship other gods. But every time they came to their senses through military defeat, sickness, or famine, and repented of their sin, God welcomed them back. Certainly God's desire was for them to radically and permanently change their way of living and focus on His ways, His love, His law, and His blessings. But change was not what happened first. It never is. Those stubborn, wayward folks had to return first, and change later. It was in the process of returning that change could occur. "If my people ... will humble themselves and pray and seek my face [first] and turn from their wicked ways [second], then I will hear from heaven and will forgive their sin and will heal their land" (2 Chr 7:14).

"Just as I am" means that God is willing to receive us the minute we admit we can't earn His love. Our hope is built on nothing less than Jesus' blood and righteousness! In *Pursuit of God*, the great A.W. Tozer wrote, "[God] is just, indeed, and He will not condone sin; but through the blood of the everlasting covenant He is able to act toward us exactly as if we had never sinned. Toward the trusting sons of men His mercy will always triumph over justice."

Are you afraid that coming out of hiding and admitting your weaknesses to God will separate you from His love? It won't. Are you afraid that admitting your inner poverty will separate you from the love of Christ? It cannot. Are you anxious over a difficult marriage, loneliness, your future or the future of your children, a negative self-image, rejection by loved ones, mistakes, failures, or uncertainty? No matter what is on your heart, it can't keep God's love at bay.

The gospel of God's grace proclaims to each of us today: Nothing can ever separate us from the love of God made visible in Christ Jesus our Lord. If that truth can't bring us out of hiding, I don't know what can!

God's Love Is Hope-Based

God shows up to encourage me in my struggle for integrity at the most amazing times. Just a couple of days after my final "confession session" with Roy, I received a call from one of the largest churches in our city, inviting me to speak to their women's Bible study. Although the idea of speaking before such a sizable group may strike terror in your heart, it absolutely turns my crank! In spite of all that had gone on in my life, there was still a live coal of desire burning in my soul to be a Christian speaker.

By the time I was fifteen years old, I knew this desire was my calling from God. He had both equipped me to respond to the call with gifts of communication and exhortation, and had created the longing for this type of ministry. Because He is committed to keeping me in line with His highest purposes, however, He had worked it so that the invitations to speak which had been so plentiful in the past had virtually disappeared into the fog of my rebellion. I believe that this particular invitation was God's precious, personal confirmation of His approval of my humbled heart. He was again ready to bless my ministry. I was elated.

When I hung up the telephone after accepting the invitation, I wept again. Not from sorrow this time, but from renewed hope. I cried as I realized God had not only forgiven my sin, but was committed to building a new future for me and for those I loved. "Forget the former things; do not dwell on the past. See, I am doing a new thing! Now it springs up ..." (Is 43:18-19).

God has outlined a specific process for cleansing and restoration. This process toward becoming real does not guarantee ease and comfort, but it does promise the precious gifts of a clear conscience, an ability to love out of a pure heart, an opportunity to develop the kind of confidence that can come only from being integrated and at peace within, and the assurance of a loving Savior who always welcomes us into His transforming presence.

Keep reading, dear friend, right through the next chapter, where the process is clearly described.

True Reflections

1. My struggle with God's unconditional love came out of my tendency to picture God in my mother's image. Have you remade God into the likeness of some person? How does that error affect your relationship with God, and how does it alter your experience of His unconditional love?

2. Do you struggle with fears of ridicule and abandonment by God? What have you (mistakenly) believed you had to do in order to retain God's love? Do you believe that God's love for you is relationship-based?

3. When you read the words "God loves you just as you are, and not as you should be," what is the immediate reaction of your heart? What areas of your life have you believed had to change before you could experience His love and compassion?

4. Set aside a few minutes right now to come to God—just as you are. Can you trust that He will meet you, welcome you, love you, and fellowship with you?

F O U R

Transformation Through Integrity

I discovered the evidence in the top right-hand drawer of his dresser. Pocket knives. Plural. Many. Maybe a couple dozen. Not the big Swiss Army type—they wouldn't fit into a seven-year-old's jeans pocket. These were the very small ones people buy as souvenirs at the gift store of a tourist attraction.

If David had been a little older, he probably would have found a safer place to hide the loot. David and his older brother, Alan, shared that room, and they knew I would be cleaning today. It was a weekly routine I dutifully performed in order to prevent being overtaken by rodents on a search-and-seizure mission to devour the remnants of candy bars, used wads of gum, miscellaneous pieces of vegetables my sons claimed to have eaten at dinner, and various other items that grew in the dark recesses of pants pockets, under-bed stashes, and dresser drawers. But David was too young to have mastered the sophisticated art of effective cover-up.

There was no question where the knives had come from. Each had a picture of a tiger on one side and the inscription "San Diego Zoo" on the other. I didn't have to be Colombo to piece together this puzzle: the day before, his class had visited the zoo on a field trip. Since I hadn't supplied him with enough spending money to fund the beginning of a massive knife collection, I knew the souvenirs were "hot." God was protecting David by keeping him from being anywhere close when I made my discovery. Had he been near at hand, he would have been under my hand! As it was, he was at school and blithely ignorant of being found out.

I bounced between disappointment, confusion, and fury. Our son, a kleptomaniac at age seven? No! Not sweet, cute, bright (of course) little David! He had been in Sunday school every weekend since he was six days old! He could put many adults to shame with the reams of Scripture he could quote! He could recite most of the Bible stories from Generations to Recollections!

But my proud mother persona quickly gave way to the sheriff within me. How could he do that? What was he thinking? Who did he think he was? Did he really believe he could hide these knives from me, his very own MOTHER?? Just wait 'til he gets home from school!

I'm too much of an action figure to sit around and wait calmly. So I did the next most emotionally satisfying thing I could think of at the moment. I called his father. Somehow Roy never seems to get quite as concerned as I do over these things. I don't understand it. But then you should know that

Roy's idea of a big night out is going to Sears to buy trash cans! That type of personality doesn't seem to react with nearly as much intensity as mine does. Following my dramatic explanation of the discovery, however, Roy surprised me by expressing some genuine concern. His quiet wisdom broke through the clouds of my growing despair and anger. "We need a plan, Miriam," he said. "I'll pray about it for a little while and call you back."

Now that's what every family needs: one partner who prays and comes up with the right solution, but who can barely muster enough energy to implement it, and the other partner who panics and wants to execute the offender on the spot. Between the two poles is the equator of balance.

Roy soon called with his very wise idea. After extended discussion and some considerable compromise, we were settled on our approach before David came home from school.

After dinner that night, as the family helped clean off the table, I said in my most casual voice, "David, I found a bunch of knives in your drawer today. Do they belong to you?" I recognized the look that came over his face. I've had that look a couple of times myself when pulled over by our local California Highway Patrol officer. The slight lift of the eyebrows indicates the initial discomfort of exposure, then terror produces temporary paralysis, followed by the sickly half-smile of cover-up. Agony is not easy to hide.

"No, Mom," he recovered. "Danny [his next-door neighbor buddy] has a collection of knives, and I just borrowed those to look at." The agony of deceit was replaced by a look of desperate hope that I would fall for this lame explanation.

"I didn't know Danny collected knives. He's never mentioned it when I've been around."

"He just started, Mom. Really. They're his."

I kept up the act a while longer. "So he is building his collection on twenty-five identical knives from the San Diego Zoo? Why would he have so many of the same kind?"

"I dunno. Ask him yourself." David's guilt was fueling his now defensive attitude.

"Well, maybe I'll just do that." The hook was set and I began to reel in my son. "I wonder if his mom knows he's interested in knives. It's rather dangerous to have a bunch of those lying around anyway. I'll give her a call when I finish the dishes."

"Go ahead," my now-cocky son encouraged. "You'll see for yourself."

Agony now gripped my own heart. Could he be telling the truth after all? Had I suspected him of something for which he really wasn't responsible? Was my son truly innocent of the charges I had brought against him? For the next fifteen minutes I kept my hands busy while my mind raced through all that had just happened.

About the time I was ready to walk into David's room to apologize, he appeared in the kitchen doorway with tears running down his precious cheeks. "Mom," he confessed, "the knives aren't Danny's. They're mine."

"Yours, David?" I continued with the obvious. "Where did you get them?"

"Yesterday, at the zoo."

I kept up the pressure. "How did you do that? Where did you get the money?"

David had come to his watershed moment—that crisis point when the offender must determine if he is going to go through with a full confession. A scene from the age-old battle between the forces of good and evil was visible on my little boy's face. All the questions that have been asked since the serpent deceived Eve in the garden were being rehearsed in his young mind: *Do I have to tell her everything? How much can I not tell and still tell the truth? Will she know that I'm lying? What will happen if I'm totally honest? Will I be punished? Will it hurt? Will she quit loving me? Will I be kicked out of the house? What will happen to me?* Other, not so obvious, concerns also entered into the decision he was about to make: *What will happen to the knives? Those are really cool knives. Will she let me keep them?*

At the instant when David precariously wavered between truth and deceit and I hovered over him, trying to find the appropriate balance between an abusive reaction and tough love, God intervened. He had been watching and waiting for this very moment. He gave David the strength to confess to stealing the knives, and poured His compassion into my heart for this tormented child. I knelt down and took my sobbing son into my arms. Through my own tears I reassured him, "It's going to be all right, David. Thank you for telling me the truth."

About that time my husband came around the corner.

"What's going on here?" Roy innocently inquired. David's pain was not over yet.

"Tell your daddy about the knives, David," I instructed. I held him as he told the story to his father. The plan Roy and I had settled on earlier in the day was about to spring into action.

"I have to tell you I'm disappointed in what you've done, Son," Roy began. "You know the knives have to be taken back to the zoo, don't you?"

David nodded, unable to control his voice enough to speak. Roy continued, "I'm going to take off work a little early tomorrow and pick you up after school. We will go together to the zoo, where you will tell the people what you have done and return the knives. Do you understand?"

More nodding and greater leaning against my shoulder. "Come on in the living room with your mom and me. There is one other person who needs to be told about this. Do you know who that is?"

"Y-y-yes," David stammered. "God."

"You're right."

The pathetic trio headed for the sofa: one very sorry little boy, an exhausted mother, and a daddy who really hated confrontations, but knew he had to see this one through. I prayed first, asking God to deal with all of us with His gentle compassion, and particularly to reassure David of His love for him. Then it was David's turn. Like his mother, David is rarely at a loss for words. But today there was neither need nor room for verbosity. Simplicity was the key: "Dear Jesus, I admit I took the knives. I know I shouldn't have done it. I won't do it again.

Please forgive me. Amen."

True to his word, Roy was waiting outside Brier Patch Elementary School at 2:20 P.M. the next day. The child known for his exuberance and many friends was quiet and alone as he walked slowly to his daddy's truck. What David didn't know was that earlier that day Roy had placed a telephone call to the head of the security department of the San Diego Zoo. Later Roy would tell me how understanding and kind the man was as Roy explained the situation.

"So you want me to ensure he doesn't do this again, Mr. Conrad?"

"That's right. Can you just put the fear of God into him without scaring him to death?"

"Well, I don't know about putting the fear of God into him, but I can assure you I can put the fear of the Security Department of the San Diego Zoo into him! You'll have to handle the religion department."

When Roy and David arrived at the zoo, they were immediately ushered into the Security Department's offices. A uniformed, armed Goliath met David and, opening a door marked "Head of Security," said, "Come in here, young man." Roy got up to go with them, and was promptly and decisively told to sit down and wait outside; this was a matter between David and the San Diego Zoo. The guard winked at Roy. It was obvious he had been through this before.

On the way home, David explained to his father that the man had been "nice, but really tough."

"You know what, Dad?" he said. "I can't go to the zoo for

a whole year, and I'm not allowed to go into any of the gift shops at the zoo until I'm twelve years old! And if I'm ever caught stealing again, they are going to call the police and have me taken to juvenile hall!"

"Is that right? Sounds like they consider this episode pretty serious business, doesn't it, Son? Do you think that's fair?"

A slight smile formed on David's face and his entire body reflected his relief as he settled down into the seat. "Yeah, Dad, that's fair. I won't like having to stay away for a year, but it's fair."

"I think it's fair, too, David."

It was over. The deceit was confessed, the punishment meted out, the offender restored and forgiven, God and the San Diego Zoo satisfied, and Roy and I pooped, but relieved.

Grown-up Deceptions

Although you have just read the true story of a young child's experience with deceit, confession, repentance, forgiveness, and restoration, the essential elements remain the same when deception is found in any of us, no matter our age. God may use any of a thousand ways to bring us face to face with our transgressions. There will come a day when He begins to direct the circumstances of our environment in order to get our attention. He will use anyone, anything, from the smallest injury to all the powers of heaven, to get His message across: "That is enough! To go on as you are will destroy you and break My heart. Stop right where you are. This very day you must face the reality of the sin in your life, admit your part in it, and either repent or face My judgment." At that moment of reckoning, all our false self-confidence vanishes, and we look truth in the eye, perhaps for the first time.

I do not mean to give the impression that I believe all Christian women are untruthful, deceptive, and untrustworthy. Neither do I mean to imply that we all have dark secrets hiding in the bottom drawer of our dresser! But I've been privileged to be in ministry for nearly forty years now, and I've spoken to thousands of women in groups and many hundreds one-on-one. As a result, I am convinced that many of us conceal secrets that need to be confessed and healed. We are not always honest about what we think and feel. We are afraid to be real.

I believe that deceit, in all its forms, is always rooted in fear: fear that who we are is unacceptable, that what we say will sound stupid, that the truth will be more painful than a lie, that God's love is not adequate to cover the complexity of our situations. Scripture provides many clear illustrations of people who lacked confidence in the plan and power of God. Taking upon themselves the responsibility to find alternative strategies to deal with their immediate pressures, each of them resorted to some form of deceit, primarily lying. The result of each incident was disaster.

Remember Abraham as he went into Egypt? He instructed his beautiful wife to lie about their relationship and say she was his sister (see Gn 12:11-20). The outcome of that lie not only brought physical suffering to all of Pharaoh's household, but I believe it altered the relationship between Abraham and Sarah from that day forward. If Abraham would lie to a stranger in order to save his own skin, would he not lie to Sarah, also, in times of great pressure and stress? Could she ever fully trust him again? There can be no confidence in any relationship unless we are assured of mutual honesty and openness.

The apostle Peter claimed to be the epitome of strength and dependability. He was going to stand beside Jesus no matter what! The only problem with Peter was that his brain forgot to tell his mouth and feet what the plan was. When the time came for Peter to live out his bold assertion, he failed miserably. He resorted to the path of least resistance and greatest humiliation: he lied and ran.

I identify with the emotional turmoil of both Jesus and Peter in that story. I have felt abandoned and betrayed by those who claimed to be true friends. I have also faced my own appalling lack of strength and integrity just at the moment I needed it most. I have, in effect, said to God, "Excuse me, I'm going off in this direction for a while; I'll check in with You later," hoping He just wouldn't bother me while I made some questionable choices. I have opted not to learn from some of my mistakes the first time and have had to reexperience the painful discipline of God. And I have learned through many bitter tears and long nights of regret that my choices affect not only me, but also my family and everything I touch. But, praise God, I have also learned that when I return to Him in repentance and sorrow, His willingness to forgive and repair situations in life-transforming ways is far beyond anything I can imagine.

The Journey Toward Integrity

Each step along the way to a life of integrity and openness is essential, but just as important is the order in which we take these steps. The process involves admitting to ourselves the whole truth and nothing but the truth about who we are, confessing our "hiding" strategies to God, changing our course through genuine repentance, and making amends to those we have harmed—all the while depending on God's power and grace to effect the kind of internal change that only He can accomplish.

Admission

Before we can confess anything to God, we must admit it to ourselves. We cannot confess or repent of something that we will not admit we have done! Attempting to discuss a matter with God that we deep down don't believe we're responsible for, or we debate is actually wrong, or we consider too insignificant to mention, is worse than an exercise in futility; it is living a lie. God knows our hearts. If we want to know the joy of sins forgiven, peace of heart and mind, confidence to face the struggles of each new day, and hope for future blessing, then we must first join the psalmist in praying sincerely, "Search me, O God, and know my heart; test me and know my anxious thoughts. See if there is any offensive way in me ..." (Ps 139:23, 24).

I struggled for so long with feelings of remorse, regret, and sorrow over my life of deception and sinfulness. For years before I confessed my sin to God or to others whom I had injured by my rebellion, I felt bad about myself and the situation I had created. I can't ever remember feeling "good" deep down in my soul during that time. Although there were happy moments, they didn't last long. Yet, even though I felt bad about my sin, and even determined to live differently, forgiveness for sin remained outside my reach—as did relief from the consequences of my behavior and restoration of fellowship with God and my family.

Alcoholics Anonymous is renowned for its members' willingness to stand, state their name, and admit their alcoholism. "Hello, I'm Jane, and I am an alcoholic." Those who have never struggled with that particular devastation sometimes mock the recovering alcoholic's bold self-revelation. But I can't imagine a more definitive moment in our journey than the one when we summon the courage to admit to ourselves, "Hello, self, this is Miriam, and I am a sinner." And then to continue, "I am not only a sinner by nature, I am a sinner by choice. I have made many choices to deceive, to hide, to rationalize, and to cover up my sin. I no longer choose to blame, to project, or to deny. I did it. It is my fault. No one else is responsible, just me." Until we can come to the place where we face ourselves in this way, in the awful blackness of our own culpability and guilt, it is absurd to proceed on to confession to God and to others.

I'm no psychologist, so I can't offer years of scientific study concerning the manner or length of time required to truly face our own souls. But for me, the length of time and the intensity of the experience involved in facing myself is directly proportional to the length of time and the amount of energy I've given to hiding it from myself! If I've only recently and "casually" told a lie, it is relatively easy to say to myself, "Miriam, you just told a lie. You are a liar. You must confess that to God. You must seek God's help in order to repent. You must sincerely and consistently depend upon His deep work in your soul to change your heart." But if, as with the credit card deception, I've spent months or years hiding not only the actual sin from my soul, but the damage it is doing to the relationship between myself and others, then admitting my guilt and becoming willing to face the consequences is slow in coming.

For weeks after it became clear to me that I wasn't going to get away with continuing my deceptive life, I struggled with the Holy Spirit as He increased the internal pressure of my guilt. I tried to construct a legitimate excuse for my behavior. I tried being nicer to Roy. I kept the house cleaner than ever. I even planned and cooked nutritionally sound and attractive meals. I spent extra time helping my boys with their homework. Absurd as it sounds, I even tried being more "spiritual." I read my Bible more, worked harder to pray through all of my daily "list." I tried anything and everything to keep from facing myself.

Then one day I hit bottom. Someone has said that the

greatest motivation for change is pain. Succinctly put, that is what happened to me. I was weary, so very weary, of all the sin, deceit, covering up, lying, and misery. My heart longed for peace, and my body desperately needed the rest of the forgiven. Whatever severe discipline, retribution, or loss might be waiting for me on the other side of facing up to my actions, it could not be as painful as living with myself every day. How deeply I felt the shame, guilt, pain, and yearning for relief that sin brought.

Centuries earlier, David the psalmist had experienced those same emotions:

Lord, my longings are sitting in plain sight,
    my groans an old story to you.
My heart's about to break;
    I'm a burned-out case ...
I'm on the edge of losing it—
    the pain in my gut keeps burning.

PSALM 38:9-10, THE MESSAGE

When I kept it all inside, my bones turned to powder
    my words became daylong groans.
The pressure never let up;
    all the juices of my life dried up.

PSALM 32:3-4, THE MESSAGE

The load of pain and sorrow in my soul was so heavy that the temptation to retreat from the task that lay ahead nearly overtook me. And so I prayed—not yet for forgiveness, but for wisdom, strength, and courage as I began to face the magnitude and awful reality of what I had done. When the agony of my own deceit became more than I could bear, it was finally over. I could speak truth to myself, even though it tore my heart out to admit it. I was finally ready to follow in the psalmist's footsteps:

> Then I let it all out,
>> I said, "I'll make a clean breast of my failures to God."
>>> PSALM 32:5, THE MESSAGE

Finally, I could approach God with the right attitude. Of course, I wasn't totally cognizant of every single infraction or hurt I had inflicted, but I was no longer in denial about what I needed to confess. I was, at last, beginning to be real.

Confession

Confession to God of the reality of our sin, whether it is a lifetime of deceit or a one-time look of lust, and the willingness to accept personal responsibility for our actions, are necessary in order to experience forgiveness and ultimate renewal of heart and mind. "If we confess our sins, he is faithful and just and will forgive us our sins and purify us from all unrighteousness" (1 Jn 1:9). Notice the big word "if" at the beginning of that wonderful promise. If we are to ever become "real" with God, we must learn to truthfully, completely, with humility itemize and specify as best we can our sins of commission and omission. Our confession should be stated in simple, clear terms that leave no room for excuses or self-justification. What specific things have I done in the past seven days, maybe in the past twenty-four hours, that were designed to cover up, to deny, to hide, to deceive? Have I told a lie? Have I lived a lie? Did I refuse to speak when truth would have been both beneficial and right? Or did I lie by my actions? Did I pretend to be something or someone I was not?

From my experience I can testify that it is far better to just "bite the bullet," name the sin specifically, and then lean back fully upon the promises of God, than to try to beat around the bush. After all, He's not fooled by our pretense. He's not impressed by our lofty words, or taken in by lame excuses. He wants "truth in the inward parts" (Ps 51:6, KJV).

"Why does God put us through this?" you might ask. Well, you can trust confidently that everything our God asks of us is motivated by His heart of love. His goal is not to make us squirm and show us who's Boss. Rather, He knows that the act of confessing our offenses is good for our soul. It humbles us and is meant to drive us to the foot of Calvary, where we can only cry out to Him for His grace, mercy, and forgiveness— which He is most eager to give in abundance. God also knows that the excruciating job of honestly confessing our sin is likely to motivate us to change our behavior!

One of the primary reasons I don't drive ninety miles per hour on the freeway is that I once had to write a sizable check because I thought I could get away with that kind of behavior. If I had just written the nice officer a lovely apology and paid for the stamp to mail it in, you may be certain I'd be far more tempted to drive at high speed again. But because there is a vast difference between writing an apology and writing a check, I choose today to alter my behavior behind the wheel because of the pain that financial penalty caused me.

You know where I'm going here, don't you? It doesn't usually feel good to say, "I lied to Joyce today, Lord," or, "I stole from the family when I charged that new outfit today, Lord." But it's not meant to feel good—at least initially. When your mother used to insist that she clean out the scrape you got when you fell down, her motivation wasn't to make you feel good at the moment, but she knew that the temporary pain of cleaning the wound would prevent more serious infection later.

Well, that's exactly what is happening during confession. If you and I submit the wounds of our soul to God with a sincere, specific confession, the Holy Spirit will use the memory of the pain that confession caused us as a tool to prevent future offense.

Repentance

After facing ourselves with the truth of what we have done, then confessing the offenses to God, it is time for the next essential step in becoming real: repentance. Attempting to reap the benefits of God's abundant mercy and grace without truly repenting of our deceitful way of life will compound the seriousness of our crimes and halt our progress toward healing and wholeness.

The definitions of repentance and confession are similar, but not the same. Confession means admitting our offense to another. Repentance, on the other hand, means determining not to repeat the offense. The repentant person must take specific and consistent steps to avoid repeating the same or similar sinful actions.

The twice-yearly sale at Nordstrom always did me in. The store opens at 7:00 A.M. on the first morning of the sale, and I was always right there at seven sharp, so they wouldn't regret their decision! But after confessing all my credit card schemes to God and Roy, I knew I needed to stay far, far away from the mall when the Nordstrom ads started arriving in the mail. On the night before the first day of the sale, I handed Roy the keys to the car and told him to take them to work with him the next day. I didn't darken the door of that store for months. No use putting an industrial-strength shopper inside the most tempting environment possible! The next time I went to the mall, I made certain I didn't carry even one credit card. In fact, Roy and I had cut all but one of them into little pieces. Then I had written letters to each of my creditors, requesting that they close my account to further charges while I committed myself to paying off the debt. All of those actions were part of my repentance. They were also part of forming new habits and learning godly discipline in financial matters.

Some say that repentance means "turning around" from the sinful direction in which one has been traveling and heading in the exact opposite direction. That is a good instruction, and easy to grasp. However, don't let the simplicity of those words make you believe that repentance is an easy task. It is not. In fact, it is virtually impossible to permanently change our ways, no matter how determined we may be, unless God intervenes and supplies supernatural strength and wisdom. The enemy of our soul does not give up tempting us just because he observes our confessions and notes our repentant hearts. In fact, our temptations might become even more intense. Evil doesn't easily relinquish its hold. Therefore, we must embrace our absolute weakness and susceptibility to even more failure if we try to live out our repentance without God's supernatural help. We might be able to temporarily generate some self-discipline, but it will never be enough to get us to the finish line. We need the loving arms of our Father to carry us over.

Restitution

Finally, we must face the impact our sin and selfish behavior have had on others around us, and attempt to make that right, as much as possible. One more time we must ask God to help us see things from His perspective. Humble, sincere apologies must be offered; restitution made, if necessary; and decisions made about our future course of action which will prevent the same type of behavior.

When I confessed to my sin of overspending, a sense of relief and peace flooded my soul. Yet I was still responsible for paying all those bills! If our local Nordstrom store manager had been privy to my story, I'm quite certain he would have been pleased at my change of heart regarding fiscal responsibility. That worthy decision alone, however, did not pay the amount I owed.

So ... Roy and I developed a very strict budget together, to which I willingly submitted. Our purchases were drastically diminished for the next year as we worked to reduce the debt. Whereas before I would have lied about our precarious financial position when Roy decided to buy a big-ticket item, now I didn't have to make excuses or even the decisions. The Conrad home was operating on a major austerity plan; everybody knew it, abided by it, and eventually benefited from it.

I was fortunate beyond words to have the support, cooperation, and forgiveness of many of the people I had harmed, but the process of making amends does not always go so smoothly. Even after you offer the most heartfelt, genuine apology, the person you have offended may not automatically offer forgiveness, or even civility, in return. But that isn't the object of confession or repentance. We don't go through all this so that in the end people will love us again, in spite of our sin, and make us feel good about ourselves. If that is our motivation, then we have just entered into a massive manipulation scheme!

God tells us to go and make it right with our brother, and so we must do just that (see Mt 5:23-26). If our brother or sister chooses not to "make it right" with us, that's his or her business, and we are released from obligation. Our "good feelings," should we experience them, come from the knowledge that our sins are forgiven and God chooses not to remember them or hold them against us.

We may live the rest of our lives learning some of the toughest lessons. Learning to be real, to be honest, to be sincere, to have integrity is neither for the fainthearted nor for the half-convinced. It is for those who wish to become more courageous than they are, more godly than they've been, and more joyful than they could imagine. Make this the day that you begin to choose integrity over deceit, reality over masquerades, and transparency over secrecy. As you do, hear these words which have brought reassurance and faith to my insecure heart more times than I can recall:

Being confident of this, that he who began a good work in you will carry it on to completion until the day of Christ Jesus.

PHILIPPIANS 1:6

Let's walk together into the light.

True Reflections

1. What methods of deception have you used to hide from God—and from people? Why are you afraid to reveal your self to God or others?

2. Every step in the journey toward integrity is necessary if we want to become "real" women. Where are you in your journey: at the step of admission, confession, repentance, or restitution? Are you stuck at any of these places?

Admission: Ask God, the Holy Spirit, to give you courage and strength to face the reality of every sin with which He wants you to deal today. Write each one down and carefully consider it individually. Remember, you don't need to deal with all your sins in one day—only the ones He brings to mind. Don't let fear or shame keep you from full obedience.

Confession: As you talk with God concerning each item on your list, accept full responsibility for your part in the sin. Refuse to let yourself blame circumstances or other people. Confess your motives as well as your actions. You will find an extra measure of freedom if you confess your sins to a trusted Christian friend (see Jas 5:16).

Repentance: As you deal with these issues, ask God to begin creating new, wholesome desires in you to replace the temptation to sin. Believe that He understands fully your weaknesses in certain areas. Search the Scripture for promises of deliverance. Stand firm on God's Word!

Restitution: This is an area where we must rely upon God for specific direction. If we don't wait for His leading, we can create all kinds of disaster by revisiting long-past issues in inappropriate ways. Some restitution is obvious, such as payment of debt, or returning of stolen goods. But when restitution involves relationship issues only, spend much time in prayer, then boldly follow God's guidance. He can be trusted to lead you every step of the way.

3. After you have worked through these steps, choose a day to joyfully and confidently *burn the list!*

FIVE

Under the Blood or Under the Rug?

I have always believed that when a woman reaches middle age, she should have found the secret to inner peace and tranquillity, to transparency in relationships, to integrity of character. She should live as an integrated, whole person.

By the time I turned fifty-five, I truly believed my life exemplified those traits. Many things were going right for me. My husband was still happy to be married to me (most days), even after almost forty years. I had not yet heard any serious discontent voiced by our adult children regarding our parenting skills. The four grandchildren God had blessed us with had already seemed to accept the fact that their grandmother was not the typical blue-haired, cookie-baking, baby-sitting matriarch, but they knew I really loved them and they returned that love.

I was proficient in many skills: I could keep a clean house; hold down a full-time, high-stress job; commute two hours a day; and still find time to make gravy for dinner! I knew how to plan a meaningful worship service, write an effective Sunday school lesson, play a flawless offertory, and lead somebody through the Four Spiritual Laws to salvation.

So why was I depressed? Where was the appalling darkness coming from that had settled deep down inside my soul? Why couldn't I locate its origin or define its form? I used every possible method I knew to dispel the blackness. I prayed long and hard. Others prayed over me, with me, for me, and about me. I tried fasting from food, feasting on the Word, contemplating and meditating while on retreat, and immersing myself in service. But my "dark night of the soul" grew like a cancer, until it permeated every pore of my being and sucked the life right out of me. My next moment of truth wouldn't wait for me to invite it in. Denial was about to be forcibly evicted from my mind, soul, and body.

Hiding From God

In Matthew 7 Jesus addresses His followers with intensity: "Many will say to me on that day, 'Lord, Lord, did we not prophesy in your name, and in your name drive out demons and perform many miracles?' Then I will tell them plainly, 'I never knew you. Away from me, you evildoers!'" (vv. 22, 23). Please note carefully that Jesus did not say, "You never knew me." Rather, He said, "I never knew you."

My intense drive to know God through the years was commendable and worthy; however, I had never realized that I needed to open myself to being known by Him. For years I had dreamed and prayed and worked toward an intimate relationship with God while continuing to wear my layers of protective stoicism and denial. Why did I do that? Why did I hide from God while running after Him? Why didn't I admit God into the deep levels of my soul, which needed His healing touch?

Because I did not fully understand His character. I had formed a God of my own twisted design, made in the image of an abusive parent. My mother never touched me except to hit me in anger. She openly confessed her hatred for me. According to her evaluation I was a bother and a constant disappointment. Specifically, I wasn't pretty, as were the other little girls in my schoolroom. Had I been prettier, she often said, perhaps she could have cared about me a little.

How easy it was for me to project my experience with my mother onto God. For years I believed that when I went to the altar in a moment of weakness and searching and didn't get totally "fixed up," He would shake His head in remorse that He had made me. Just as I was an embarrassment and disappointment to my mother, so I was to my God. Now I know that is a lie, but the road to truth has been rocky.

As an evangelical, born-again, full-time speaker, musician, wife, mother, and grandmother, I spent more than five decades of my life denying the pain that my mother's attitudes and actions had inflicted on my soul and spirit. Oh, I could easily talk about her rejection when I was asked to give my testimony. Stoic and dry-eyed, I would relate many heartbreaking instances of both emotional and physical abuse as well as neglect and abandonment. My listeners would weep because I had touched some very sensitive areas in their own hearts, and also because they sympathized with my pain (which I did not feel myself).

My denial drove me to work at a frenzied pace in order to avoid being still long enough to allow the pain to catch up with me. For far too many years I poured the abject despondency of my relationship with my mother into some black space in my heart. I thought I was throwing it away, but that wasn't the case. Long after her death in 1969 I continued to subconsciously attempt to make myself worthy of her love. And because deep down I knew I could never succeed, I held back the wounded part of myself from the heavenly Parent I believed would ultimately reject me as well.

The Christian community has never agreed on how to deal with the issue of denial as it relates to past wounds. Some wonderful Christian leaders claim there is no hope for any long-term effective ministry by those who refuse to painstakingly review the events of their childhood or other periods of trauma in order to deal with all residual effects. Other wonderful Christians confidently quote the apostle Paul to verify their belief that it's never necessary to "look backward," that we should only "press on toward the goal to win the prize" (Phil 3:14).

I believe that in between those two extremes is balance. Hiding behind our painful memories and using those events and issues as excuses for stunted personal or spiritual growth and integration back into healthy relationships is a common tragedy. However, if we consistently deny the real impact of those same experiences and feelings, and fail to bring them to Jesus, we can never be forgiven, cleansed, comforted, or made whole.

No matter what our age or what the source of our suffering, pain eventually gets our attention. We can deny or medicate it, ignore or tolerate it, but pain is relentless. Whether emotional or physical, distancing ourselves from pain buys time, but not solutions. For me, the pool of darkness inside eventually became deeper than my reservoir of superhuman strength—the pseudo-strength with which I held back the internal barrage of painful memories. My Abba, my loving heavenly Father, desired "truth in the inward parts" (Ps 51:6, KJV). He was standing by His promise to complete the good work He had begun in me (see Phil 1:6). And to do that He had to forcibly remove my ability to hide, deny, or suppress all those memories.

The tool He used was clinical depression. For several weeks I cried nonstop and felt indescribable hopelessness. Although ignorant of the cause, Roy recognized the symptoms and enlisted the help of our friend, Judy, to convince me to seek treatment.

The Meltdown

The long, dim hallway seemed to go on forever. As I stumbled around a corner, my eyes froze on the brass-edged black sign:

PSYCHIATRY. I collapsed on the floor. Roy reached down and took my hand as my dearest friend knelt on the floor beside me. "Come on, Miriam, we'll help you. It's not too much farther."

Everything in me wanted to find strength enough to run back to the car, but there was no reservoir from which to draw. I was empty. I was dry. For the first time I had lost control. There would be no running away now. Decades of denial had forced me to this place and there would be no escape.

By this time I had been crying steadily for several hours, so you can imagine my swollen eyes, smeared mascara, and nose the size and color of Vermont in the blaze of autumn! My panic immediately began to dissipate, however, as the receptionist treated me with respect. I'm not sure what I expected to find once we walked through the frosted glass doors—certainly not what I did discover. The normalcy of the environment got my immediate attention. It was just another waiting room, well lit, with regular people waiting for their appointments in regular chairs. I'm certain I stared much too long at the individuals who made up this temporary community of shared pain.

"Mrs. Conrad," the voice behind me called. I looked around to see a tiny lady waiting for me in the open door. I grabbed both Roy and Judy anxiously, and the three of us walked behind the doctor down another long hall to her office.

Dr. Snow began probing gently about what was troubling me. After asking Roy and Judy a few questions, she excused them, and I was left alone with the doctor, my wringing hands, and my abject hopelessness. We talked for an hour. She kept smiling. At first I wasn't sure if the smile was for her benefit—a mask behind which she could hide her real concerns or maybe irritations at such a weak patient. But soon enough, the Holy Spirit helped me realize that Dr. Snow was smiling for my benefit, to reassure me of what she'd already concluded early in our conversation: my situation was far from hopeless. There was help available for me—both immediate and long-term help—if I was willing to accept it.

"Miriam, if you had come in here with diabetes and I asked you to take insulin every day for the rest of your life in order to ensure good health, would you do it?"

"Well, of course," I answered.

"How about if you had a severe case of pneumonia and I gave you penicillin. Would you faithfully take the medication in order to get well?"

"That's a no-brainer. Obviously I would take the cure. What's your point?"

"Well, Miriam, you have a chemical imbalance in your brain, and I want to give you medicine to help regain that balance. The medicine is commonly known as an antidepressant. Will you take it?"

Suddenly all the religious training I'd had, the caustic comments from other Christians, and the things I had read about how Christians didn't need psychiatric help came rushing like a flood through my brain.

"No, Dr. Snow," I blurted out. "I can't take that kind of medicine. I'm a Christian, and I'm not supposed to need that kind of stuff. I have Jesus in my life, and He can fix this."

Patiently she responded, "Oh, I respect your religious con-victions very much, Miriam, but think again about what we have just discussed. You remember you said you would agree to treatment for the illnesses of diabetes or pneumonia. What you have now is an illness in your mind. There is safe and spe-cific treatment available. We will keep careful watch over you for the next few weeks. Please, won't you give it a try?"

I was too weak to fight her rational thinking and nodded my head.

Judy and I waited in the car as Roy picked up the prescrip-tion at the pharmacy. When we got home and I got settled in bed, Roy came in with the first dose and a glass of water. He sensed my apprehension and began to pray a prayer I repeat silently every day as I continue to take the medicine: "Dear Lord Jesus, if there is anything that is good for Miriam in this medication, please help her body to absorb it. If there is any-thing here that would harm her, just allow her body to flush it through. We trust you to know the difference. Amen."

As I swallowed the medicine, I knew that along with the yet-unresolved pain that had brought me to this place, I faced the embarrassment of having finally "broken down." I was one of those women who had to take pills to remain stable. And unless God chose to radically change my situation, I would need help for the rest of my life. Suddenly I was no longer the strong, self-sufficient person I had believed myself to be. Was this to be the end of ministry as I had known it? If the word got out that I had experienced a "meltdown" (Roy's preferred terminology), would my speaking engagements be canceled? Would I ever be asked to minister anywhere again? Were the problems and pain that had used up all the mood-stabilizing chemicals in my brain now gone forever? On this medication would I just coast through life in some foggy trance? Would I lose "me" in all this?

"Oh God, oh God," were the only words of prayer my heart could form. I soon knew that they were more than enough.

The cords of death entangled me;
the torrents of destruction overwhelmed me.
The cords of the grave coiled around me;
the snares of death confronted me.

In my distress I called to the Lord;
I cried to my God for help.
From his temple he heard my voice;
my cry came before him, into his ears.

PSALM 18:4-6

I discovered that there is, for the very weakest and least powerful among us, a unique level of grace available. Listen again to the psalmist:

God, the one and only—I'll wait as long as he says.
Everything I hope for comes from him, so why not?
He's solid rock under my feet, breathing room for my soul,
an impregnable castle: I'm set for life.

My help and glory are in God—granite-strength and safe-
   harbor-God—
so trust him absolutely, people;
Lay your lives on the line for him. God is a safe place to be.
                                       PSALM 62:1, 2, 5-7, THE MESSAGE

Deliverance

The very next day I began, for the first time, to live my life one
moment at a time. Long-term plans and goals were temporarily
abandoned. Minute-by-minute dependence upon God became
my mode of operation for several weeks. Looking directly to
Him for answers to all my questions was the only choice I had.
I willingly stepped down from my "take charge" platform and
allowed God and others to lead me along.

During the next six months of my recovery, I began to
admit what an expert I had become at denying my pain. I discovered that it is not only those who carry great loads of sin
who are destined to eventually collapse under the weight of it
all; the same may be said for those carrying the heaviness of
sorrow and despair. The terror and humiliation of a physical
collapse, psychological breakdown, or emotional meltdown
may be what God uses to snap us out of our denial and self-
sufficiency. In order for Him to rebuild us from the inside out
and establish our footing on the Rock, He must remove all the
castles we have built on sand.

Although my anxiety decreased over the weeks as the medication restored the flow of seratonin in my brain, I was still faced with resolving the issues that had brought me to despair in the first place. And so, after a few weeks, I took the next step by seeing Claire, a Christian therapist. I couldn't begin to describe all the ways God has used Claire to point me to spiritual, emotional, and physical health, but I do want to tell you about one very important session.

Soon after I began seeing Claire, she asked me to write down my story of growing up in my family of origin. Because of the volatile nature of that story, it took us several appointments to read through it together. For the first time I was actually experiencing the cumulative pain and hurt I'd experienced during my childhood. As I talked to Claire I would cry openly and sometimes uncontrollably. Often she would interrupt me to say things like, "That was absolute cruelty," or, "It's a miracle of God that you didn't end up permanently locked in the loony bin," or, "I am so sorry, Miriam, that must have really hurt."

Eventually we made it through to the last page. I can point to the exact spot in the parking lot where I stopped dead still as I walked to my car. Something was missing. Was it my purse? No, it was hanging on my shoulder. Was it my glasses? No, they were on my face. I had my keys in my hand, so I knew I hadn't left them in Claire's office. What was it that was missing?

I walked unsteadily to my car with the nagging thought that I was leaving something important behind. Not until I got home and began reflecting on that day's session did I realize what was gone: the trunk. The trunk I had carried for years, full of secret hurts, sorrows, questions, and disappointments. Every once in a while I would try to open the trunk and take out one of the objects—perhaps a memory of Mom's anger or Dad's passivity—and hope that someone would *see*, realize the depth of my pain, and acknowledge that I had a right to cry. Sometimes I would take the objects out and show them inappropriately—to a stranger who would listen, or an audience that might care, or a friend who might be able to help. But each time I would realize they either couldn't or wouldn't heal me, and so I would put the object back in the trunk and go into hiding once again. I had carried that heavy, pain-filled trunk all my adult life. But now it was missing. Gone. The absence of heaviness was beyond argument. I knew it was part of my past. It truly felt like a miracle.

As I continued to think about what had happened that afternoon, the Holy Spirit opened my eyes to the truth: I had finally opened the trunk all the way. At last I had forsaken every denial tactic I had so carefully mastered. In the safety and security of Claire's office, I had let her—and God—see all the way inside my soul. And rather than dismiss my pain as trivial, insignificant, or something that should have been forgiven and forgotten years ago, God used Claire to speak His words of understanding and compassion like a balm. "Yes, Miriam, that really did hurt. It was not right, much less fair. Your mother was cruel and your father abdicated his responsibility to the family. You have truly suffered and I am so sorry for your pain."

The denial was no longer necessary. The trunk had vanished. Oh, I still remember the past. And sometimes it still hurts. But it just isn't "heavy" anymore. I'm not bent over with anguish. I'm no longer exhausted from the search to find someone who will understand and care. God delivered me from my dungeon of despair and continues to teach me that healing is a process. Life is a process. Holiness is a process.

The Healing Path

My earliest memories recall ministers, including my own daddy, urging those in the congregation to "Come, leave your sins and your burdens at the altar." There is such a finality and closure implied in those words. And if the ministers refer only to what God will do for us when we confess our sin, certainly they speak gospel truth. God can be absolutely depended upon to forgive and forget our transgressions. "If we confess our sins, he is faithful and just and will forgive us our sins" (1 Jn 1:9). But often the implication seemed to be that not only every sin, but also every burden of our hearts, would be "rolled away." When we stood up from our knees, if we had "done it right" at the altar, we would be completely free not only from the punishment we deserved for our sins, but from any lingering doubts, any residual emotional damage, certainly any bondage to destructive habits or recurring temptations.

I resolutely believe in the miracle-working power of God to instantly and entirely deliver people from any besetting sin or burden, and I have personally witnessed repeated examples of those whom God has miraculously set free from destructive habits or overwhelming oppression. Scripture repeatedly affirms God's deep desire that our encounters with Him radically alter our character and actions. "Therefore, if anyone is in Christ, he is a new creation; the old has gone, the new has come!" (2 Cor 5:17). However, while God is able, willing, and often does choose to immediately change us at the moment we seek Him, sometimes (and I believe most of the time) it's not nearly that simple or quick. I repeat: of course, any sin issue is resolved. We are forgiven. God has chosen not to remember. But we cannot forgive or forget nearly so easily. The healing path God designs for us to walk in order to find freedom, light, and hope may not be so smooth.

If we believe that all negative emotions are to be "left at the altar," what do we do when we find our hearts heavy again in a few hours? What are we to think when the old pain, shame, temptations, doubts, and questions return to haunt us? Of course we are not powerless against the enemy of our soul, who would continually accuse us and try to negate the work Christ has done. We may confidently claim the precious, powerful Word of God to effectively deal with Satan. But some issues in our lives don't need to be cast out, they need to be brought up! They need to be admitted, verbalized, and committed to God's healing care over and over again, no matter how long it takes!

Jesus said, "Come to me, all you who are weary and burdened, and I will give you rest. Take my yoke upon you and learn from me, for I am gentle and humble in heart, and you will find rest for your souls" (Mt 11:28-29). Note that physical rest is not the goal; spiritual (soul) rest is the essential need. Our souls need to lay down their burdens—over and over and over again. There is no implication in Jesus' words that we are to come to Him only once per issue, never to have to face the problem again.

Expecting new or even mature believers to experience immediate and complete resolution to every painful situation is to lay on them a horrible additional burden. For those of us who need to be delivered from a performance-based relationship with God, the addition of guilt from not being instantly "fixed" is overwhelming. Anyone would praise God for the precious gift of a godly family and the lasting effects of love, security, and affirmation. We would expect the impressions made upon us in those formative years to positively influence our personalities, choices, relationships, and even career decisions as long as we live. How strange, then, that those of us who were not privileged to be born into such a loving atmosphere, but one of pain and rejection, are often expected to deny or "get over" the reality of the fallout of those negative years and act as if they never happened.

Frederick Buechner writes in *The Clown in the Belfry,* "We are never more alive to life than when it hurts—never more aware both of our own powerlessness to save ourselves and of at least the possibility of a power beyond ourselves to save us and heal us if we can only open ourselves to it." Opening ourselves to pain involves leaning into our emotions, our circumstances, our hurts, and our hopes, and walking through our pain to the healing on the other side. Pain, particularly emotional pain, is often the seedbed of sanctified discontent, providing the inner momentum to move us out of ruts, damaging relationships, and destructive situations. Pain is a catalyst for action.

Fortunately, for me, pain propelled me into positive action in the form of seeking medical and psychological treatment, which removed the final barriers to profound spiritual healing. My recuperative process has been neither quick nor simple. In fact, it continues to this very moment. But the results have been glorious—and that word doesn't begin to describe the difference. To face the reality of pain, but not wallow in it. To admit and confess the anger without living in blame. To forgive the people who hurt me without condoning their actions. To let go of hatred as I attempt to understand the causes of my mother's own pain. To weep openly when telling my story because I truly remember how badly all that hurt. To bring to Jesus the lingering questions for His solutions and healing.

I believe one of our greatest challenges as Christians is to understand and live out the two seemingly paradoxical commands in Philippians 2:12 ("continue to work out your salvation with fear and trembling") and Philippians 3:13 ("forgetting what is behind and straining toward what is ahead"). Actually, it isn't nearly as hard as it seems (truth is generally simple). We just need to use the same biblical principle we apply to many other areas of our lives—that is, we do our part and God does His.

Our part is to be honest about our life experiences, neither denying them nor using them as crutches on which to lean a victim mentality. Until God has been given permission and opportunity to reveal the lessons we are to learn from those experiences, the wounds will never heal. God's part is to forgive our sin and to bring good out of bad, ultimately healing our emotions and equipping us with compassion for others who have experienced similar hurts.

My journey toward understanding these principles has been arduous, and I am so grateful that some of the rockiest road is behind me. I pray that you will learn, much more easily and quickly than I did, that trusting God to take care of what's "under the blood" doesn't mean we are to shove everything else "under the rug." When we get these thoughts straight in our mind, then we can rest assured that His blood has cleansed the stain of every confessed sin, and that He will provide wisdom, strength, and hope for the memories and issues we must face. We need not live in denial of whatever is troubling us. There is a balm, there is healing and rest when we lay our burdens down at the feet of Jesus.

True Reflections

1. Why has denial seemed more comfortable to you than facing the truth? Who or what has encouraged you in your denial?

2. Can you name some past experiences which bring pain or humiliation when you think about them? Have you ever brought these incidents to God for healing? Have you covered up all or part of your emotions because of fear of facing them?

3. Perhaps you have brought these incidents to God prior to today. How many times do you think God is willing to discuss them with you?

4. Do you think you will know when true healing has taken place? How?

SIX

Between Covering Up and Throwing Up

As important as it is to learn not to hide, to be vulnerable and open before God and trusted others, we must be careful not to swing too far to the other extreme. Once we begin to experience the exhilarating freedom of laying down our burdens and relinquishing our hiding strategies, it's tempting to throw open the floodgates and "let it all hang out." But a woman of integrity and transparency is also a woman of wisdom and discernment. She doesn't lead a life of duplicity, but she doesn't blurt out everything she thinks, either. And she doesn't welcome the whole world into her inner sanctum.

When I worked as an administrator, one of my goals when hiring was to find people who evidenced good, old-fashioned common sense. Trying to teach a person sensitivity or discernment, much less the glorious trait of godly wisdom, is a real challenge. I have found that godly discernment is never more necessary than when engaged in conversation. Charles Dyer, author of *The Power of Personal Integrity*, illustrates my point all too clearly.

> Gaius: *Good morning, Rufus! I didn't see you before the service began today. Say, has anyone been honest enough to tell you how hideous your new toga looks? It reminds me of something I would buy from a tent-maker rather than a seamstress. Of course, you have been gaining weight, so maybe it is best to try to hide everything.*
>
> Rufus: *Why, thank you, Gaius! By the way, I've been meaning to tell you how obnoxious I find your wife and children. I don't know how you ever plan to marry off those two homely kids.*

A determination to come out of denial in order to become authentic and transparent needs to be worked out within the framework of discretion and propriety, and certainly under the guidance of the Holy Spirit. We all know those who never share their feelings, failures, struggles, or dreams. Their extreme self-protection insults and mystifies us. Equally disconcerting are those who consistently embarrass everyone around them by "spilling their guts" all over the floor at every opportunity. Those in the latter group inevitably gravitate to public places—specifically my speaking engagements.

I just love it when people make the heroic effort to fight the current of departing women in order to come down front after an event to talk with me personally. Well, most of the time I love it. Somewhere in the middle of the line is usually a woman who just can't wait to throw up her story of woe. When it is finally her turn to shake my hand, she approaches with a measured step and martyr's smile and offers a limp handshake. "I felt every word you spoke tonight," she begins. "You see …" and she's off and running, delivering a speech she has obviously prepared during the last half of my presentation. She begins by recalling stories of her mother's prenatal illnesses, details every event of her troubled childhood, and, given the slightest encouragement, continues with a blow-by-blow description of her rotten marriage or the heartbreak her foolish children cause her. Totally oblivious to the number or needs of others who unfortunately find themselves behind her in line, she lays it all out, from the mundane to the gory.

The consequences of not knowing when to speak and when to keep silent can be much more than irritating, however; they can be devastating. Consider the story of Samson and Delilah. Samson was the strongest man the world has ever known. He could have won every "Mr. Universe" pageant with no sweat (pun intended). His bronzed muscles rippled under the light weight of his toga. He was undoubtedly the first Terminator! But this incredibly powerful man had a glaring weak point. It was the muscle hinged between his palate and his lower jaw. His tongue, though small, was about to overpower every other developed muscle, ruin his reputation, and destroy his life.

When we enter the story, Sam has fallen in love with a woman named Delilah. I imagine women were falling all over themselves to get Sam's attention, so we can assume that Delilah was an outstanding beauty. However, that gorgeous body housed a mercenary mind and a treacherous heart. Delilah had entered into an agreement with five Philistine men who were Samson's archenemies. Her assignment was to discover the secret of Sam's strength, remove it, and render him helpless.

Can't you just see it? Here's Delilah, perfumed and definitely dressed to impress. Samson comes in after a long day at the office and just wants a little peace, quiet, and loving conversation. He probably thinks that her inquiry about what gives him his strength is a seductive tease, so he responds with a really absurd answer: "Tie me up with seven fresh thongs that haven't been dried and I'll be putty in your hands, girl." Unaware of his deception, she takes him seriously and sends the Philistine Phive out to the local Thongs R Us for the freshest ones they can find. While Samson sleeps she ties him up, believing that this is going to be her moment of glory. Unfortunately for Delilah and her gang, when she wakes Samson, he breaks the thongs like thread and goes about his business.

This game-playing went on for several more days. Samson allowed himself to be tied up with new ropes, which he summarily snapped like spaghetti, and one night even had his hair braided into a loom that was permanently attached to the floor. That time he pulled the loom right out of the floor. I would guess he looked a little silly ... the Terminator with a loom for a hairpiece.

You may be assured all this was not making Delilah a happy woman. She not only had her reputation as Sam's best girl on the line, but several hundred silver shekels, promised upon completion of her evil deed. As is often the case with a woman scorned, she began to rage internally and pout externally. Something would have to be done to convince this man to spill the truth. You'll never convince me that Scripture is dull. Listen to this account:

> Then she said to him, "How can you say, 'I love you,' when you won't confide in me? This is the third time you have made a fool of me and haven't told me the secret of your great strength." With such nagging she prodded him day after day until he was tired to death. So he told her everything. "No razor has ever been used on my head," he said, "because I have been a Nazirite set apart to God since birth. If my head were shaved, my strength would leave me, and I would become as weak as any other man."
>
> When Delilah saw that he had told her everything, she sent word to the rulers of the Philistines, "Come back once more; he has told me everything." So the rulers of the Philistines returned with the silver in their hands.
>
> Having put him to sleep on her lap, she called a man to shave off the seven braids of his hair, and so began to subdue him. And his strength left him. Then she called, "Samson, the Philistines are upon you!" He awoke from his sleep and thought, "I'll go out as before and shake myself free." But he did not know that the Lord had left him.

Then the Philistines seized him, gouged out his eyes, and took him down to Gaza. Binding him with bronze shackles, they set him to grinding in the prison.

JUDGES 16:15-21

So much for living an open and authentic life in community!

In Search of Balance

So what is the balance? Does God expect us to show and tell everything, in the name of honesty and integrity? How can we be transparent without being foolish? How can we protect the privacy of family and friends while learning to be authentic ourselves?

In his book *Integrity*, Stephen L. Carter sums it up well:

You don't have to tell people everything you know. Lying and nondisclosure, as the law often recognizes, are not the same thing. Sometimes it is actually illegal to tell what you know, as for example, in the disclosure of certain financial information by market insiders. Or it may be unethical, as when a lawyer reveals a confidence entrusted to her by a client. It may be simple bad manners, as in the case of a gratuitous comment to a colleague on his attire. And it may be subject to religious punishment, as when a Roman Catholic priest breaks the seal of the confessional, an offense that carries an automatic excommunication.

Recently my husband and I were discussing how we have watched the evangelical church go through some significant changes over the past four decades, particularly in the area of sharing problems, weaknesses, victories, and strengths. When Roy and I were first married, more than forty years ago, we attended Wednesday evening prayer meetings at church where it was common to hear people volunteer "unspoken" prayer requests. The specific nature of the issue was not revealed, so when the group began to pray it was somewhat a case of "the blind leading the blind." Of course, God knew all of our hearts and honored our sincerity in prayer. But as I reflect on those times, I realize we were emotionally isolated from each other in the name of "privacy." There was no vulnerability or point of connection. If Roy and I were struggling with one of our children and never felt free enough to share that, we also were not in a position to receive wise advice and practical support from others who had walked the same road before us.

Then we came to the sixties—the years of communal living and "letting it all hang out." As is generally the case, the church took what it liked from the current culture of the world, modified it somewhat, and then began to use it. So we were urged from the pulpit and by the respected authors of the time to begin to open up, be more communicative with each other, and leave our secrets behind. I attended prayer meetings during those years where "unspoken" prayer requests were not allowed. If you wanted prayer for something or somebody, you had to clearly articulate the problem so that we could "pray with wisdom."

Then in the seventies and eighties we were exhorted to engage in the supercharged (and supposedly biblical) activity called "confrontation." Prayer groups took on the dimension of self-help programs as entire evenings were given over to addressing the problems of the first person who was unlucky enough to share that night. If someone garnered sufficient intestinal fortitude to mention that he or she was wrestling over an issue as benign as purchasing a new car, then we all began to offer our "spiritual insight" regarding the lack of importance of temporal possessions, the scriptural principles for handling finances, and even the direct question, "Why not fix the car you've got and give the rest to missions?" Loving confrontation about vital issues was soon replaced by criticism of minor things, until suddenly we would come to our senses and realize we had only five minutes left to pray!

In the nineties, the people of God seem to be returning to balance. We are beginning again to appreciate the wisdom of not speaking to the masses about everything that's on our hearts, but we're also more willing to share honestly those things that bring us grief and pain. The women I admire deeply and whom I would call women of integrity have learned the skill of effective and prudent openness. They have mastered the ability to say just enough, at just the right time, to just the right people by allowing the Holy Spirit to speak directly to their hearts at all times, warning, correcting, encouraging, silencing, or whatever is appropriate at the moment.

It is an ongoing goal of mine to be so in tune with the Lord Jesus that He can either slap His hand over my mouth to shut me up or instantly open my heart and loose my tongue so I can minister more effectively. Let me outline for you my three guidelines to effective and appropriate sharing. They are designed to help you comfortably walk that tightrope between covering up and throwing up.

Check Your Motivation

Most of us love to talk about ourselves. Human nature drives us to be recognized, to be admired, even to be pitied. Certainly there are situations where crying out our need is appropriate. Let me remind you of the story of blind Bartimaeus:

> As Jesus was leaving [Jericho], trailed by his disciples and a parade of people, a blind beggar by the name of Bartimaeus, son of Timaeus, was sitting alongside the road. When he heard that Jesus the Nazarene was passing by, he began to cry out, "Son of David, Jesus! Mercy, have mercy on me!" Many tried to hush him up, but he yelled all the louder, "Son of David! Mercy, have mercy on me!"
>
> Jesus stopped in his tracks. "Call him over."
>
> They called him. "It's your lucky day! Get up! He's calling you to come!" Throwing off his coat, he was on his feet at once, and came to Jesus.
>
> Jesus said, "What can I do for you?"
>
> The blind man said, "Rabbi, I want to see."
>
> "On your way," said Jesus. "Your faith has saved and healed you."
>
> In that very instant he recovered his sight and followed Jesus down the road.
>
> MARK 10:46-52, THE MESSAGE

Bartimaeus' yelling out at the top of his lungs, drawing the attention of the entire crowd, including Jesus, was the perfect method for this unique situation.

On the other hand, here is a story of a person healed while trying her best to remain anonymous:

In the crowd that day there was a woman who for twelve years had been afflicted with hemorrhages. She had spent every penny she had on doctors but not one had been able to help her. She slipped in from behind and touched the edge of Jesus' robe. At that very moment her hemorrhaging stopped. Jesus said, "Who touched me?"

When no one stepped forward, Peter said, "But Master, we've got crowds of people on our hands. Dozens have touched you."

Jesus insisted, "Someone touched me. I felt power discharging from me."

When the woman realized that she couldn't remain hidden, she knelt trembling before him. In front of all the people, she blurted out her story—why she touched him and how at that same moment she was healed.

Jesus said, "Daughter, you took a risk trusting me, and now you're healed and whole. Live well, live blessed!"

LUKE 8:43-48, THE MESSAGE

These two stories illustrate the distinct differences in the way you and I may evidence our need, or even our stories of recovery. Each person involved used the appropriate method for obtaining the results they desired. Please note this very significant truth, however: in each case, it was not the method, but the motivation, that Jesus responded to. Blind Bartimaeus screamed to get Jesus' attention; the bleeding woman pursued Him silently. But drawing attention to themselves was not their ultimate goal. Their aim was to encounter Jesus, the only one who had the power to fix their problem. Jesus was their focus, and so it should be with us. Not our methods, not our stories, not our sufferings, but our Savior.

There is such a temptation to share things for their shock value, such as how sinful or victimized we have been in the past. How many times have we heard someone tell his or her story with twenty-five minutes devoted to sin and five minutes to redemption? We must ask ourselves, "Why am I talking about this?" Our "before" stories may be interesting and dramatic, but nothing about our own history is going to redeem the soul of any other person. The redemption comes in their hearts, as it did in ours, with the knowledge of the work and person of Jesus Christ.

On the other extreme, we may believe our good reputation depends upon our keeping silent, maintaining an untarnished appearance, and never opening ourselves up in order to receive or to offer help. Our motivation in this case is fear and lack of trust in the omnipotence of God to ultimately maintain our cause. The truth is, we can't continue to mask our hurts and struggles forever. They come out in illnesses, wrinkles, and bad dispositions. We need the wisdom, comfort, encouragement, and accountability that living in community with others provides.

Ultimately we must learn to recognize the voice of God through the prompting of His Holy Spirit. Only then can we be assured that our focus is on target: the redemptive work of Christ in our lives.

Assess Your Environment

In 2 Kings 18-20 we are told the story of King Hezekiah, one of the very few good kings to reign in Judah. Listen to what the Bible says about God's servant Hez:

> Hezekiah trusted in the Lord, the God of Israel. There was no one like him among all the kings of Judah, either before him or after him. He held fast to the Lord and did not cease to follow him; he kept the commands the Lord had given Moses. And the Lord was with him; he was successful in whatever he undertook.
>
> 2 KINGS 18:5-7

During Hezekiah's lifetime he experienced miraculous deliverance from his enemies, including witnessing the angel of the Lord put to death 185,000 of his adversaries in one night! Then one day Hezekiah got some terrible disease and the prophet Isaiah came to tell him to put his house in order, for he was about to die. Hez didn't give up easily, however, and, while in his bed, turned over to face the wall and began to plead with God: "Remember, O Lord, how I have walked before you faithfully and with wholehearted devotion and have done what is good in your eyes" (2 Kgs 20:3).

God heard—immediately. And before Isaiah had a chance to get out of Hezekiah's palace, God told the prophet to go back and tell the king that he was going to live another fifteen years.

You would think that a king with that much faith in God's ability to defend, provide, and heal would have instinctively learned somewhere along the line a good deal of wisdom and godly discretion. Well, if you think wisdom automatically comes along with faith, you're naive. Listen to what happened to unwise King Hez in the very next verse.

Soon after this, Merodach-Baladan, son of Baladan, king of Babylon, sent Hezekiah his best wishes and a gift, for he had heard that Hezekiah had been very sick. Hezekiah welcomed the Babylonian envoys and [watch out here!] showed them everything in his treasure-houses—the silver, the gold, the spices, and the aromatic oils. He also took them to see his armory and showed them all his other treasures—everything! There was nothing in his palace or kingdom that Hezekiah did not show them.

Then Isaiah the prophet went to King Hezekiah and asked him, "What did those men want? Where were they from?"

Hezekiah replied, "They came from the distant land of Babylon."

"What did they see in your palace?" Isaiah asked.

"They saw everything," Hezekiah replied. "I showed them everything I own—all my treasures."

2 KINGS 20:12-15, NLT

I can just imagine Isaiah standing there shaking his head in disbelief and disappointment.

"Good grrrrrief, Hezekiah! What were you thinking? Those 'visitors' were the Babylonian KGB! You just gave away every secret you have about the location of Fort Knox, the intelligence of the Pentagon, and how to invade Judah at its most vulnerable spot."

2 KINGS 20:16-18, *my translation*

At this point the great King Hez slinks away into oblivion. In spite of great victories in battle and a glorious touch from God in the healing of his body, Hezekiah failed to assess his environment when it came to interacting with these VIPs. My guess is that, like many of us, King Hez became just a little cocky after all the good treatment from God, and began to think he was somehow special. Perhaps he thought nothing would prove that better than to show off some of God's blessings (giving Him adequate glory during the tour, of course).

But Hezekiah was so wrong. He had no idea what was in the hearts of those men. He could not have known what they would do with this information. And neither can you or I unless we consult God before we tell all. If Hezekiah had asked for guidance and discernment before he threw open the doors of his kingdom, God would have gladly instructed him to keep his mouth shut and would have urged him to send those wicked men home without the tour! Hezekiah's righteous kingdom would have endured.

Our kingdoms may not consist of vast stores of gold and silver, spices, and armies. They might best be described as storehouses of precious, private experiences with God. They are our treasures, and they are priceless to us. We may have important things to say and a desperate need for someone to listen, but sometimes we choose the wrong environment in which to share what is close to our hearts.

In order to discern whether it is safe and wise to share, ask yourself a couple of questions in order to size up your environment: "Do I have the right to speak in this context?" and "Do they need to hear what I have to say?" If the woman in line at my speaking engagement had asked herself these questions before she began to "spill," she probably would not have been summarily cut off from sharing with me. If she had asked me for an appointment, or found some other manner of speaking privately for a longer period of time, I would have been happy to accommodate, if my schedule permitted. In that environment, however, she did not have the right to make everyone else in line wait for twenty minutes while she went on and on.

Many of us have caused ourselves embarrassment and heartache by saying the wrong thing to the wrong person at the wrong time. With the intimate guidance of the Holy Spirit, however, we can learn to assess our environment and expose our heart's treasures only when it is both safe for us and valuable to others.

Listen to the Holy Spirit

When we are given the opportunity to share, we need to be so tuned into the voice of God in our spirit that we immediately recognize His traffic signals. Are we to keep going or stop?

When the green light says go, then *go!* He can take even stumbling words spoken with trembling lips and create a life-changing message. When He says, "Say it!" then don't grieve Him by keeping quiet. That moment can never be reclaimed, once lost. Trust Him. He will not allow you to go out on a limb and then cut it off behind you.

Several years ago I was asked to be a seminar leader at a conference where many world-class speakers were being featured. Knowing that the women who would attend my seminar would be fresh from a session with one of these famous people was enough to give definition to the phrase "scared spitless." As I began, my mouth was so dry that my words appeared to be creating a dust cloud in the room. Still, God quietly urged me to keep on going. This I did, with the tape recorder over in the corner silently preserving for posterity the tremble in my voice and the knocking of my knees.

You know what? That tape is now my biggest seller! More women have written to express appreciation for that message than any other I've ever recorded! Just this year a dear friend who teaches the Bible better than any woman I've ever heard, told me this: "Miriam, when it's anointed, it's fun. When it's hard, it's obedience." She's right.

On the other hand ... think about the potential disaster if we run God's red light. Collision, injury, destruction, or even death can be the result. Just as God knows our hearts, He also knows the hearts of our listeners. He knows their motivations, is well acquainted with their character, and looks into the future to see what they will do with the information we provide. He knows it all; we don't. We may think we know people, but so Samson thought he knew Delilah.

The principle is that it isn't enough just to be an honest person. We must also be people of discernment and discretion. Our relationship with God, the Holy Spirit, must be open enough to hear His warnings and direction. I would venture to bet that when Delilah first asked Samson about the secret to his strength, God whispered in Sam's ear, "Watch out, boy. The source of your strength is a matter between you and Me. Let's keep it that way. Keep your ears and eyes open and your mouth shut."

God is aware that some people could be trusted with the formula to Coca-Cola and they would never reveal one element. He also knows that some people can hardly be trusted with your e-mail address! Regrettably, you and I are not privy to that kind of knowledge, so we must learn to listen carefully to the whisper of the Spirit within.

As God provides supernatural sensitivity and the discretion to know when and with whom we should share, we may still have questions about *why* we should share our weaknesses with others. Read on, because that's exactly what we're going to talk about in the next chapter.

True Reflections

1. If asked, most of us can recall someone who fits the description of "lack of propriety" in sharing environments. In your

opinion, what is it that motivates such people to inappropriately "spill their guts"? How can you help such a person achieve balance and discretion?

2. Try to remember the last two or three times you were in a group where sharing was encouraged. In those situations did you find you tended to talk too much or too little? When you walked away, did you feel embarrassed at dominating the conversation, or did you regret not participating more? What specific actions can you take to bring your own participation into balance?

3. This chapter offers three guidelines to help us share effectively and appropriately:
   • Check your motivation.
   • Assess your environment.
   • Listen to the Holy Spirit.

   Which of these do you struggle with the most? Would you be willing to ask a friend to hold you accountable for putting each of these into practice at your next sharing opportunity?

SEVEN

ℰℊ

Trophies and Scars

When my father was a young man, he traveled the East Coast and Midwest with a group of Shakespearean actors, entertainers, and debaters known as the Chautauqua Circuit. In his late twenties he embraced the Christian faith, and eventually graduated from Moody Bible Institute as a minister of the gospel. However, he didn't leave all the trappings of the stage behind. Into the pulpit came an imposing figure with all the flair for the dramatic that had made him such a success in his former vocation. Familiar Bible stories left his listeners rapt and wide-eyed. Daddy was loud, sometimes long, but never dull!

The chances that I would inherit a ton of genetic dynamite were pretty high. You've already read a little bit about my mother. Emotionally driven and mentally unstable, she added more than a normal share of sensational genes to Daddy's dramatic ones. I've been told I'm forever perched precariously on the knife edge between greatness and disaster! An enthusiastic, dramatic extrovert to the core, I love celebrations, Disneyland, audiences, and especially surprises (nice ones, of course).

These aspects of my inborn character are what God uses to make it such a joy for me to stand before crowds and tell women about Jesus. People often ask if I am nervous just prior to speaking. Not at all. By the time I get to the event I'm like a racehorse at the gate: just open it up and let me run! Yet, these same character traits make the potential for pride, self-centered speaking, unnecessary embellishment, and downright lying a real temptation.

In my quest for authenticity and integrity, is my ultimate desire to live and to tell a self-centered story, or a God-centered story? Is my goal to proudly display the trophies of my achievements (giving some credit to God, of course)? To salaciously expose my gory wounds to the "oohs" and "aahs" of an awe-stricken audience? Or am I willing to humbly expose the divine Surgeon's handiwork on my soul—scars and all? The bottom-line question is, do I want people to look and listen to me and say, "What an amazing woman!" or "What an amazing God!"?

Amazing Grace

Lisa had been asked to speak at our Professional Women's meeting. Her presentation was unforgettable.

"I really don't know how many times I've been arrested,"

she began with a half-smile. "Maybe six or seven. I lost count after the first three or four times. You've seen people like me many times on TV, holding our anti-abortion signs and screaming 'Baby-killer!' and 'Jesus loves you' in the same breath.

"I was raised in an atmosphere of activism. My parents have always been politically involved, consistently on the conservative side of issues. Demonstrating to emphasize our views was just a normal part of life. Certainly our values included being pro-life, and so during my college years I often found myself debating in classrooms during the week and picketing abortion clinics on the weekends. When it came time for me to write my master's thesis, I determined to focus on the abortion issue. In order to fulfill the requirements for this paper I directed several comprehensive studies which centered on the negative residual effects of abortion for the mother, as well as the actual physical pain the fetus suffers during the procedure.

"Academically and intellectually I was probably as well informed on this topic as anyone in my city. I continued to publicly display my distaste for those who would perform abortions, and attempted many times to interfere with those entering the clinic for treatment. That's when I would be arrested. However, no matter how well I knew the facts or could quote statistics, and no matter how willing I was to be hauled off to jail for my stand, I am sad to say I don't remember ever truly influencing one single person to change her mind about going through with the procedure.

"The summer following graduation, my parents encouraged

me to take a few weeks off from all responsibilities before I began working. They generously funded a trip overseas and I spent three weeks lounging around on the most beautiful island beach you can imagine. Those weeks changed my life forever. Alone and totally 'free,' I somehow lost my bearings. I began to drink heavily for the first time and to hang out in the bar right on the beach.

"One morning, just two days before my vacation was to end, I woke up in a strange hotel room, lying naked beside a stranger. Evidently I had become so drunk the night before that I had willingly come to this man's room, and only God knows what all happened before the dawn came. I was scared to death and vowed to pack my bags and sit in my room weeping and praying until my plane left the next day.

"On the way home, I wept again, so regretting my actions, and grateful that I could escape the environment in which I had become so lost. Returning home to my parents, my friends, my new job, my own apartment, and my church was comforting beyond words. After a few days I was able to reflect on my island experience with regret, but the shame certainly didn't immobilize me from getting right back into the swing of things.

"About six weeks passed before I began to suspect anything, but a home pregnancy test revealed my worst fear: I was pregnant. For a few days I thought I would literally go crazy. About three days after the discovery, however, I woke up in the middle of the night with the most incredible thought: I could have an abortion and no one would know, get hurt, or condemn me. The irrationality of my seeking an abortion when I had spent so much of my life fighting that very evil was stuffed too far down for me to consider. My own relief and anticipated peace were all that mattered.

"I made an excuse for going away for a couple of days, and flew to an abortion clinic I knew about in Atlanta. It was a quick, simple, fairly painless procedure, and I was home the next day, still the same old me, at least on the outside. I told absolutely no one.

"The responsibilities of my new job served as a perfect excuse for not getting involved in any further anti-abortion activities. As time passed, the whole horrible situation seemed more and more like a bad dream, and after a few months I hardly thought about it at all.

"Meanwhile, I met Terry, 'the' man of my life. He was a wonderful Christian, a college graduate, a member of my denomination, and a gentle spirit. The more serious we became, the more pressure I felt to tell him about the abortion. Finally, one night as we sat in my apartment, I decided that living with the guilt was too much, and I was determined to not allow this secret to be between us all our lives. He was hurt when I told him, but he was also understanding and forgiving. He did, however, have one specific response. 'You must tell your parents. Your relationship with them will never be right until you do. They love you as much as I do. It may take them a while, but they'll eventually understand. I really want you to tell them. In fact, I'll go with you when you do.'

"I was horrified, but I knew Terry was right. We made an

appointment to see my parents the next evening. I know now that my dad thought we were coming over so Terry could ask for my hand in marriage. Getting engaged is still a pretty formal thing in the South. This made the real reason for our visit even more shocking.

"Mom reacted much as I thought she would. She was surprised, confused, and hurt that I hadn't told them sooner, but willing to hug me and work through all the questions that would follow. But Dad was a different story altogether. As surprised as they were at my confession, so I was at his reaction: angry, defiant, unforgiving, and relentless in his name-calling. He told me to get out of the house until I was invited back.

"Suddenly I was on the other side of a situation I had thought I knew all about. Instead of standing outside a clinic and screaming 'baby-killer!' to the young women going in, I was the one being called a baby-killer! Added to the guilt I had been carrying for so many months, this new hurt and shame were nearly too much to carry. The daddy I loved so much turned his back on me, and with a vengeance.

"For nearly two years my father didn't speak to me. He refused to come to my wedding. Terry stood by me as I confessed, finally, my sin to God and began to receive the healing that only His precious Holy Spirit could bring. It was a very, very difficult time.

"One day my mother called and asked to take me to lunch. We had remained in contact, although the relationship was strained. During the meal, Mom said she had a suggestion that she hoped I would consider. 'Lisa,' she said, 'I've watched you suffer for two years now, and I think it's time for your grieving to take a positive turn. Why don't you begin volunteering once in a while at the Alternative Pregnancy Center downtown? No one would know better than you how those girls are feeling. You've been right where they are. You know the pressure they're under. You know they don't think there is any other choice for them. And you know personally the results of making the choice for abortion. I'm certain you could make a real difference and God could greatly use you there.'

"Although I had a hundred reasons why her suggestion was irrational for me, God knew this was exactly what I needed to do. And so began my steadily increasing involvement with a storefront, alternative pregnancy counseling center, until today it is my full-time job.

"You know something, ladies? I don't think a single one of the young women with whom I counsel every day cares one whit that I have a master's degree in psychology. Not one of them has ever asked about my academic qualifications. When I was lecturing to the masses and picketing outside the clinics, I was asked that question many times: 'What qualifies you to speak on this issue, or to take such a radical stand?' I was always proud to point to my studies, my achievements, and my knowledge. But it never seemed to change anyone's mind. The people to whom I pontificated were still skeptical, and the young women still streamed into the clinics right past my signs and my screams.

"Today, when asked my qualifications, I point to a broken heart, a compassionate spirit, an intimate understanding of their terror, and the possibility of healing and renewal in spite of the enormity of their situation. And every day I see lives changed. Incredibly difficult decisions are made which will alter consciences and emotions forever. Not one of those hurting women wants to see my trophies. All they're interested in are my scars."

Lisa allowed the discipline of God and the excruciating pain of her experience to mold her character from the inside out, to equip her to extend the amazing grace she had received to other women who needed it desperately. She could have chosen instead to remain in hiding, or even to boast about the miracles God had done in her life. Fortunately for her, her husband, and many women at a crossroads, Lisa chose to cherish her scars and let God use them for His glory.

Divine Surgery

Certainly if anyone had reason to build a room to display his life-size trophies, it would have been Jesus. He made the blind see and the crippled walk, He raised the dead and healed the sick, He redeemed the most blatant sinners and penetrated the hearts of the self-righteous. Jesus deserved every accolade this world could offer. What He got instead were scars—scars received at the hands of unbelieving, undeserving, power-hungry people who were crazy with jealousy and fear.

Most of us don't go around exposing our scars. Take my husband, for example. He has had far too many surgeries to count. In one of them it was necessary to take a piece of his right hip bone and relocate it in his neck. This procedure gave new meaning to "The hip bone's connected to the neck bone!" As a result, he has quite a scar on his hip, as well as one in the front of his neck, from one ear to the other. Then just a couple of years ago he decided to knock on heaven's door again by donating his body to a vicious gall bladder episode. After they had completed that surgery, he ended up with a scar on his chest that looks like the infamous "bell curve." Since that time he has been a little more reluctant to put on his bathing suit and join the rest of our generationally-challenged neighbors in water aerobics for senior citizens.

Trophies are presented in the ecstasy of crowds and cheering. Scars, on the other hand, are received in awful silence. No one knew this better than Jesus. However, it was Jesus' scars, far more than His miracles, that changed the world forever. His scars stand as evidence of His all-consuming love for each of us.

The truth is that scars reflect much more important happenings than do trophies. Not only physical scars, but spiritual scars allowed by a loving God who operates on our souls without regard for our immediate comfort, but with a commitment to preparing us for our ultimate destiny. Our eternal holiness is far more important to God than our immediate happiness. He loves us so much that if we will submit to the knife of His redemptive surgeries, He will expertly remove our sin, repair our broken hearts, and replace our hopelessness with His joy.

Often the surgery done by our loving Father is not elective. We may go into the operating room with Him, but not willingly. Strapped down to the gurney of circumstance and pain, we fight the very process that will bring about recovery. But He knows best. And just as I once held my precious little son down as the doctor removed a deep splinter from his hand, so the Holy Spirit of God often holds us immobile so that we can't fight our way out of what will ultimately bring healing and joy to us and glory to Him.

In the Old Testament, the prophet Jonah experienced some nonelective divine surgery. Well settled in Jerusalem, probably busy in his own ministry, Jonah was called by God to the very wicked city of Nineveh to preach repentance, or severe judgment if the residents didn't repent forthwith. In order to escape the call and run from God, Jonah got on a ship headed in the exact opposite direction. Because of a terrific storm which God sent, the sailors realized that somebody, somewhere on that boat must deserve punishment. The lot fell to Jonah, and they threw him overboard in order to save their own lives.

Now, at that point, Jonah might have expected to be a goner. But no, something actually more terrible—and wonderful—than the relief of an instant drowning was about to happen to him. God caused a very large fish to swallow the prophet, and for three days and nights Jonah had the ultimate in an "up and down" religious experience! Without books to read, a bed to sleep on, a TV to watch, or friends with whom to communicate, Jonah was slapped upside the head with the absurd reality of his situation. Knowing full well what had gotten him into this predicament, Jonah realized the futility of arguing with God about Nineveh or anything else. For the time being, God had

Jonah's full attention. Against his will, of course, but nevertheless ...

When God knew Jonah was ready to listen—and to obey—the fish spit him up again on dry land. At that point the Lord came to Jonah for the second time, telling him to go to Nineveh. Jonah went, preached, and everyone in the large, very wicked city repented. God's wrath was averted.

Have you ever had a "belly of the whale" experience? I have. Sometimes it's sickness, sometimes loneliness, sometimes exhaustion, sometimes financial reversal. I've never chosen to dive into a stormy sea, hoping to be swallowed by a great fish. Personally, I've always thought I could learn my lessons just fine while sitting on a deck chair in the sun, thank you. But there are some things that can't be learned in the lap of luxury. We are going to go "down in the belly" once in a while, and when we're "spit out" onto solid ground again, we are left with tender places that remind us of God's redeeming work.

Although the results of divine surgery are magnificent, God's scalpel produces scars. This is good. You see, the courage to be real does not come by human achievement, but from the settled knowledge that God alone can make us who we are meant to be. The things we accomplish on our own, and for which we receive applause and recognition, pale in importance when compared to the truth that we are children of the Most High God.

But it is so easy to get everything backward. Personally, I've never met anyone who has chosen 2 Corinthians 11:21-27 as his or her life verses. Why? Well, I'll let you decide as you read them:

Since you admire the egomaniacs of the pulpit so much (remember, this is your old friend, the fool, talking), let me try my hand at it. Do they brag of being Hebrews, Israelites, the pure race of Abraham? I'm their match. Are they servants of Christ? I can go them one better. (I can't believe I'm saying these things. It's crazy to talk this way! But I started, and I'm going to finish.)

I've worked much harder, been jailed more often, beaten up more times than I can count, and at death's door time after time. I've been flogged five times with the Jews' thirty-nine lashes, beaten by Roman rods three times, pummeled with rocks once. I've been shipwrecked three times, and immersed in the open sea for a night and a day. In hard traveling year in and year out, I've had to ford rivers, fend off robbers, struggle with friends, struggle with foes. I've been at risk in the city, at risk in the country, endangered by desert sun and sea storm, and betrayed by those I thought were my brothers. I've known drudgery and hard labor, many a long and lonely night without sleep, many a missed meal, blasted by the cold, naked to the weather.

THE MESSAGE

There are plenty of impressive facts presented about Paul in those verses. If he had related those horror stories without underscoring the ultimate work God did in his life, his tale would have little or no value. There would be no reason for us to even want to identify with him. But listen to this: "If I have to 'brag' about myself, I'll brag about the humiliations that make me like Jesus" (2 Cor 11:30, THE MESSAGE).

Now there's a statement worthy of attention! Paul transformed his negative experiences by viewing them in light of what they accomplished in his spirit and for his Savior. So it is true for us, that our accomplishments are not of themselves of any value in the telling, unless God somehow is glorified as we share. Then our trophies become the wounds healed by His touch. Our scars display the grace and glory of God.

True Reflections

1. When you reflect on testimonies you have heard, what parts do you remember—the "trophies" (either positive or negative), or the "scars"? As honestly as you can, evaluate which portions of those same testimonies brought glory to God versus glory to the speaker.

2. Have you ever been asked to give your testimony? Did you choose to do it? Did you spend more time displaying your "trophies," or your "scars"? Did you refuse to share, thinking you had nothing to say?

3. Whether or not you have ever publicly told your story, would you be willing to share the next time you're asked?

4. I suggest that you sit down right now and write out—whether for the first time or for the one hundredth time—your own priceless God-story. Ask God to help you reveal just the right number of both your "trophies" and your "scars."

EIGHT

ᆳᆱ

Everybody Needs a Tonto

Since our children were all born within twenty-five miles of the Pacific Ocean, it was part of our family tradition to take them regularly to the beach each summer. We have enjoyed literally hundreds of evenings with a tiny, portable barbecue, hot dogs wrapped in flour tortillas (don't knock it if you haven't tried it!), chips, and Kool-Aid.

It was especially wonderful to watch Christopher, by far our most experiential child, as he had his first exposure to the ocean, to the waves, to the strange sensations of wet sand on his chubby feet. He was generally ecstatic just being in the environment, with so many new sensory experiences to be had for the taking. For the first ten minutes he just ran as fast as his short legs could carry him, up and down, parallel to the water, full of bravado and freedom.

Suddenly, a tiny, cold wave, not more than an inch or two deep, caught him by surprise, breaking over the top of his warm little feet. A scream erupted that was heard in Houston! But, just as quickly, the water retreated and immediately Christopher's confidence returned. The look on his face indicated he truly believed he had conquered the great ocean!

Voluntarily now, he inched toward the water rather than running parallel to it. He watched as the water came toward him again, lost his nerve at the last second, and ran like a cheetah in a futile attempt to make it to dry land before the cold water caught his toes. By this time a grin split his face horizontally, replacing the fear of his first encounter with the water. A game of tag ensued, the water relatively predictable in its ebbs and flows, Christopher braver and braver until he finally found himself standing in ankle-deep water, King of the Ocean!

Without warning, the Ocean pulled a fast one on the little kid. An "enormous" wave, about knee high, unexpectedly came from nowhere, knocked Christopher down on his bottom side, and all at once the game wasn't fun anymore. Terrified at the betrayal of the ocean to not stick to the rules the King had determined, he ran to me, crying for comfort and a warm, dry towel. Many, many minutes passed before my little boy was willing even to stick a toe into that great big ocean again.

When it comes to admitting our need for open, integrity-based relationships, many of us would prefer to run alongside the ocean of humanity rather than dive in. We may have spent our entire lives believing that the best way to interact with people is to wade ankle-deep in the tide of friendship, because that presented all the risk we were willing to take.

Besides, we tried getting deeper into the water once and then here came a big wave of unexpected demands on our time, or worse yet, a riptide of betrayal and misunderstandings and we had all we could do to get out of that water and onto the warm, familiar sand of independence.

For many years, psychobabble has attempted to convince us of the danger of admitting our raw need for meaningful relationships. Independence has been extolled as the epitome of mature development. To admit need was to admit weakness, to acknowledge inadequacy, and—most dangerous of all—to permit entrance by another into the most private and vulnerable parts of our souls.

Well, I strongly disagree. The older I get, the more I realize how important other people are to me and how much I need them in my life. Integrity and transparency depend upon community for expression. I suppose that's why there is so much in Scripture about helping one another, being patient with each other, caring for others, and encouraging others. Long before any of us figured it out, God filled His Word with guidance and instruction on how to relate. We were built for relationship.

Once more we turn to God's Word for ultimate truth, and Jesus is always the best example of all. What comfort and reassurance it is to watch the all-powerful God, in human form, choose not to model independence, but dependence. Jesus often declared His total reliance on God for everything He needed for life and ministry. For Jesus, dependence was a virtue, not a weakness. "The Son can do nothing by himself;

he can do only what he sees his Father doing, because whatever the Father does the Son also does" (Jn 5:19). As if that weren't clear enough, a few pages later He makes His point directly: "Apart from me you can do nothing" (Jn 15:5).

Not only did Jesus choose to teach and model dependence upon God, His Father; He also made certain we understood our need for one another. Jesus demonstrated how this type of mutual reinforcement was supposed to work when He went to the Garden of Gethsemane on the night before His death. He identified the three disciples whom He believed would stand by Him in this appalling hour of inner conflict. He took them with Him into the inner part of the garden and asked them to pray for Him as He went ahead to pray alone. The anguish Christ endured during the hours to follow had to have been intensified by the awareness that not only did His friends fail to pray, but they considered their own comfort (sleep) more important than intercession for their Master. Not only was Jesus open about His deep desire for support and companion-ship during this crisis, but He also was unashamed of His dis-appointment and sorrow when they failed Him.

Do we assume such arrogance as to think we are created to be any less dependent than the Son of God Himself? God's plan is for us to be as connected to each other as we are to Him. None of us were designed to be Lone Rangers. I used to be so impressed ... that white horse, the mask, silver bullets, black boots! Wow! What a guy! I remember the day it dawned on me that even the Lone Ranger wasn't a lone ranger. Beside him was Tonto! Even the Lone Ranger had a friend. I realized that everybody needs a Tonto because everybody needs others in their lives for support, companionship, and encouragement.

Eternal-Value Relationships

The question *Why do we need each other?* may appear too obvious on the surface to address, but it is not. We need to talk about this subject in the light of our desire to be confident women of integrity and transparency. From the moment God declared, "It is not good for the man to be alone" (Gn 2:18), His plan for us was that we would provide for each other in myriad ways.

One friend is not enough to provide all of the following essential ingredients for healthy growth:

Demonstration. We are to model for each other a Christ-like life: "Be an example to all believers in what you teach, in the way you live, in your love, your faith, and your purity" (1 Tm 4:12, NLT).

Interpretation. When we're confused by life, others can step in to help us understand. "Plans go wrong for lack of advice; many counselors bring [understanding]" (Prv 15:22, NLT).

Cooperation. We are to weep with those who weep and rejoice with those who rejoice. "When others are happy, be happy with them. If they are sad, share their sorrow" (Rom 12:15, NLT).

Affirmation. When one of us is resisting growth, another can encourage us to welcome change. "The Lord's servants must not quarrel but must be kind to everyone. They must be able to teach effectively and be patient with difficult people. They should gently teach those who oppose the truth. Perhaps God will change those people's hearts, and they will believe the truth (2 Tm 2:24, 25, NLT).

Confrontation. We are to correct one another with a gentle spirit and humble confidence. "Brothers and sisters, we urge you to warn those who are lazy. Encourage those who are timid. Take tender care of those who are weak. Be patient with everyone. See that no one pays back evil for evil, but always try to do good to each other and to everyone else (1 Thes 5:14-15, NLT).

Do you have people in your life who provide these essentials? I know from personal experience the challenge it can be to gather such a group around you. But I have also learned that God will gladly provide "Tontos" for His children who humbly ask for them. In our search for what I like to call "eternal-value relationships," we must allow God to pick and choose the person or people who will best minister to our needs. Chances are we will be surprised, not only by the particular people chosen, but by exactly how God chooses to use them in our lives.

We all have rough edges that need to be sanded off. My only problem with this process is the people God chooses to use as sandpaper! I was amazed to discover that when I finally got serious and began praying for God to surround me with people who would hold me accountable and confront any potentially dangerous direction in which I might be headed, He actually did send people! But NOT the ones I would have chosen.

I'm discovering that most of the time the people God uses for sandpaper in my life are those I don't think have the right to comment on my spiritual walk, my ministry, or my relationships with my family. When they gently but firmly express some concern, my defense mechanism launches its most powerful missiles! *Just who do you think you are? You have no right to speak to me this way!* Those are the things I want to scream, but I have learned through bitter tears and grave hours of regret that I must listen, and listen carefully. I have learned the hard way that "Wounds from a friend are better than many kisses from an enemy" (Prv 27:6, NLT). A friend tells you what you need to hear, even if the truth hurts.

I was flattered and pleased recently when a beautiful, gifted young woman came to me and asked if I would be willing to meet with her occasionally for the purpose of mentoring and "building my life into hers." Because I felt the tug of God on my heart to respond, and because I had the time, I accepted the invitation. This precious Christian lady is just beginning a speaking ministry, and as we met for the first time over lunch, I tried to respond with warmth and wisdom to the questions she asked about what was involved in staying attuned to the Holy Spirit while pursuing a ministry that would honor God.

As we were about to leave I said, "Julie, the next time we meet, I want you to bring your calendar with you and let me have a look at it." For just an instant there came over her face an expression of surprise and defense. But then she broke out into a big grin and said, "You don't mess around, do you? You go right for the jugular. I'm not so sure I want to show it to you, but I guess that means I should."

Do you know the reason I asked for that particular privilege? Because it has been one of the most problematic areas of my own life. I've always maintained that control of my time is my business, especially any free time. Picking and choosing my times and places for ministry has been one of the last fortresses of resistance against suggestions offered by Roy or others who have expressed concern. If I am not getting sick, not sloughing off at work, or not being unpleasant at home, then why should anybody question my excessive involvement, particularly in ministry?

Well, I'll give you a couple of good reasons. First, almost any excessive behavior, whether it's continually knocking your head against a brick wall, eating too much, or never taking time for adequate rest and reflection, is indicative of some type of disordered thinking. I only came to acknowledge that truth after I was forced to sit still for seven months while God commanded my full attention and "talked turkey" to me about my life and work. During those long weeks of isolation and questioning, several godly women friends called, wrote, and dropped by. Because the radical change from a job, lots of ministry travel, much social interaction, and general busyness to day after day of quiet sitting and contemplation was proving so difficult, I complained about it to anyone who would listen.

Without exception my friends told me they understood my frustration and acknowledged how difficult it must be for me. And I felt better … momentarily. But then there came words of caution: "Miriam, these days of rest are a great privilege. Use them wisely." Or words of wisdom: "Miriam, open your heart to God's Word and His presence so that He will be all you need." Or stronger words: "Miriam, what are you afraid of? Why can't you sit still? You've been running like a locomotive all your life. Allow yourself this time to refuel." Or outright confrontation: "Miriam, these very days are ordered by God. I sense that you are unwilling to cooperate with His plan for you right now. What will it take for you to submit to His very best, even though it is not what you would have chosen?"

Slowly and painfully, I began to hear the words of my friends more clearly than the squawking of my rebellious mind. Their questions became my heart's questions: "Am I open to the teaching of the Holy Spirit of God?" "Am I afraid to be still?" "Will I willingly submit to His best for me, even though I don't understand?" And the insights began to come—also slowly and painfully.

As I have come out of this particular valley, I look back on those days with deep gratitude for a God who surrounded me with just the right people. I'm certain I would be struggling with those very same issues today, had I not been gifted with true saints who loved me enough to tell me the truth at the risk of subjecting themselves to my anger and rejection.

I have recently made an amazing discovery: The word *saint* is not found in the translation of the Bible which I am currently reading. It is always "saints." Where saints are concerned, there has to be more than one. I think that divine revelation specifically teaches that it is in the very interaction we share with one another that saints are produced.

Jesus With Skin On

If we have no opportunity to be dishonest or deceitful, then there is no need for this discussion. But we don't live in isolation. Daily we interact with diverse groups: the strangers who tally and bag our groceries; the small, superficial work-group at the office; the more friendly gathering of parents at our children's school. Then we move into the places where we sense we ought to truly "belong": church congregations, large or small, and the microcongregations (i.e., the choir, Sunday school classes, small study groups). In each of these social groupings God intends for us to be "Jesus with skin on" for the building up of His body. The principle is taught in 1 Corinthians 12. Although we all belong to the same body, we each have a different function. Each of us has a part to play; each of us is necessary to the operation of the kingdom in this world.

If we are to stay healthy enough to fulfill the unique role God has designed for us, then we must surround ourselves with other women who love us enough to call us to accountability and integrity, who will identify our pride, our independence from God, our overcommitment and questionable decisions and actions. Our subtle determination to distance ourselves from those who desire our holiness even more than our happiness is one of the first signals that we may be wandering into dangerous territory.

From personal experience I can tell you how devious Satan is as he attempts to make us believe we are above the very spiritual principles and core values that we claim to embrace. Like the bad guys who hide in canyons to ambush the Lone Ranger, devious and dangerous representatives of evil lurk along our path, hoping to overtake us with their deceptions. "I deserve a little happiness" (flirting); "Why not, it's on sale" (stealing from the family budget); "I just bent the truth a little, no harm done" (lying); "I'm sorry, we'll have to eat take out again tonight, I've got (choir practice/Bible study/missionary meeting/Sunday school council/recovery program/PTA/workout session/grocery shopping/ad infinitum)." When our loving, but jealous God observes us succumbing to such dangerous temptations, you can bet your silver bullets He is going to round up some Tonto who will head into town and get help from the local posse, if necessary, in order to run off the bad guys.

Of course, we could stand our ground and pretend we can pull off the escape by ourselves. We might (and we often do) deny that there are really any bad guys out there at all, and feel that Tonto is worrying for nothing. We might (and we often do) overestimate our store of ammunition and be overwhelmed when we find ourselves empty of any strength for defense. We might (and we often do) underestimate the value of the posse God sends as reinforcements against the enemy of our souls. We might (and we often do) find ourselves in the dust of shame and regret because we refused the heavenly hosts who came in human form to help us fight the battle.

The world has looked on in cynical amusement as some Christian leaders have been revealed as maverick rebels against God's clear standards for personal integrity. Circumstances created the opportunity for me to know one of these leaders personally. I watched with increasing horror as the individual compromised her personal purity, then publicly defended her right to happiness, and finally lost all credibility and ministry as she chose momentary comfort over eternal joy. As much as I would have liked to say "That will never happen to me," you have already heard my story and know that I, too, got caught in the very thing I so vehemently decried. In retrospect, the only difference I can see between me and that former leader is that when God's posse came around in the form of a loving, godly couple who confronted me with my sin and its consequences, I accepted their help, repented of my sin, and presented myself for long-term spiritual restoration. Please know that I am not saying this out of any sense of pride; I am fully aware that it was God who was working in me, giving me the desire to obey Him, and the power to do what pleases Him. He gets the glory for all the right decisions I've made, and I get the blame for all the stupid ones!

God never intended that we would always have to figure out the answers to our problems all by ourselves. In fact, He exhorted us through Paul, "Let us not give up meeting together, as some are in the habit of doing, but let us encourage one another—and all the more as you see the Day approaching" (Heb 10:25). He never planned that we would face our struggles alone. Rather, He intended that when we faced issues that were difficult and we felt like we were in the desert of life, right beside us would be someone else. Someone to help us find direction, someone to offer words of encouragement, or someone to help fend off the bad guys.

My guess is that as you go hi-ho-silvering your way through this life, you will probably encounter a desert or two. There may even be a bad guy now and then. You've only got so many silver bullets. When your gun is empty, "It's you and me, Kemosabe." That's why it's so crucial to choose to involve yourself in relationships that invite mutual encouragement, honesty, transparency, and accountability. For those who have chosen a life of integrity, these elements are crucial. The love, reproof, stimulation, and warnings of others are essential to keeping us balanced and on track.

I know from personal experience the temptation to stay away from people when in the heat of some personal battle. Facing others can be traumatic, and running away by sitting at home seems such a logical answer. But we can never see things from a clear perspective when looking through only our own eyes. We desperately need the input and prayers of others who care for us and can offer alternatives to what appears to be so one-way.

Your confidence as a woman of God will be enhanced by those who encourage your goodness, support your righteous decisions, care enough to express concern, and provide a human safety net in case of failure. "As iron sharpens iron, a friend sharpens a friend" (Prv 27:17, NLT). A true friend will sometimes cause friction and sparks in your life, but the results are always positive. Welcome the Tontos God graciously sends to walk alongside you. To live with integrity in a corrupt world requires a little help from your friends.

True Reflections

1. Eternal-value relationships are those which contain one or more of the following:
   - Demonstration (p. 137)
   - Interpretation (p. 137)
   - Cooperation (pp. 137-38)
   - Affirmation (p. 138)
   - Confrontation (p. 138)

   Can you identify people in your life who provide all of these essentials? Which ones are not provided in any of your friendships? How do those missing relationship ingredients evidence themselves in your life? Pray earnestly for such friendships.

2. Have you ever experienced a prolonged period of forced inactivity? As you reflect on that time, how were you different at the end from how you were at the beginning? During those days, of what value were your friendships, your "Tontos"?

3. Who are the bad guys lurking in the canyons of your life to do evil? Are you being attacked by pride, selfishness, dishonesty, or moral compromise today? Are you willing to ask your Tonto to come and help you fight off the enemy? Will you accept and act on his or her advice?

℀

Get a Grip—This Ain't Eden!

There it was, right in front of my face: the latest in a series of tests God was placing before me to see if I would live out the kind of integrity I claimed to value. In a fit of spring-cleaning I discovered what I had thought was lost forever: a perfect circle of tiny diamonds, blue topaz, and gold. I'd purchased the lovely ring many years before and then, I had fully believed, left it in a hotel room in Nashville in 1996. So fully convinced had I been that it was gone forever, I had submitted a claim to our insurance agent and received payment for the treasured piece of jewelry.

Now it wasn't lost after all. It was found, in the bottom of a drawer that obviously hadn't been cleaned out in much too long!

Good grief! Now what was I to do? I picked up the ring and took it into the living room to show Roy. He looked at me with a grin on his face and said knowingly, "So I guess you have to make a telephone call tomorrow morning, eh?"

As I thought about it during the night, I had visions of the insurance company being so flabbergasted that anyone would be so honest as to say they had found a lost item, that they would just tell me how wonderful I was and to forget repayment. Wrong. The call was quickly transferred to the "I once was lost, but now am found" department, and the young man proceeded to tell me I could make restitution in either one or two payments. I chose two.

I do love the ring, and I'm very happy to be able to look down at it on my finger, but, honestly, I had gotten quite used to the fact that it was gone forever, and if you would have asked me before I found it if it were worth the several hundred dollars that would be required to bring it back, I would have quickly said, "absolutely not." Right now I'm more interested in paying the bills than decorating the fingers! That choice, however, is no longer available to me. Finding the ring meant facing my ongoing vulnerability to the temptation to be deceitful. Would I report the recovery, trusting God again for sufficient financial provision to cover what I owed?

That experience was a spiritual "reality check" for me. I needed to be reminded that living a godly life doesn't always mean being rewarded with a smooth path. In fact, sometimes circumstances only get worse! The belief that getting ourselves right with God and people will secure a carefree future is heresy. Committing ourselves to a life of integrity, transparency, and accountability is no automatic protection against even greater challenges. Many of us spend enormous amounts of energy trying to regain a lost joy (Eden) or searching for a Nirvana of peace and contentment (heaven). Yet the sooner we can settle our minds and hearts down into the truth that we are currently living on that vast plain between Eden and heaven, and that this life is not supposed to supply all the joys and glories of either one of those perfect environments, the better off we'll be!

Living East of Eden

You'll get no argument from me about how tough life is. In fact, you'll get no argument from God. Someone has said that God promises His people four things: peace, power, purpose, and trouble! As we find the courage to be real and to live out personal integrity, we gain boatloads of the peace, power, and purpose part. Like it or not, however, we also get our share of trouble. As we become sensitized to the lack of honesty everywhere around us, it's easy to become disheartened. In our attempts to be open and transparent, we are sometimes criticized, misunderstood, and rejected. As we confess our failings and move through repentance and restitution, we might have to endure heavy blows to our pride or our pocketbooks. Submitting to accountability in relationships is, more often than not, the path to brokenness.

But life isn't meant to be all gloom and doom, either. In fact, there are a few very wonderful things that life in this old world offers that Eden couldn't provide and heaven isn't going to give us! For instance, it's only on this earth that Christians have the priceless privilege of bearing testimony to Jesus Christ in the midst of a difficult and sometimes dangerous environment. When we get to heaven, everybody will be loving the Son of God; there won't be anybody denying Him or blaspheming Him. It is only here and now that we can choose to be true to Christ in the midst of the majority who are not true to Him.

Second, it is only on this earth that we have the glorious opportunity of demonstrating the power and love of the Christ who can save our souls and change our lives. When we get to heaven, there won't be any more twelve-step groups, for there will be total healing. There will be no halfway houses, for our lives will be completely holy. There will be no hospitals, or jails, or cocaine, or heroin, or mental health facilities, for we will finally be whole. But meanwhile, it is only now that those of us who have experienced some of the sorrows of a life invaded by drugs or depression or addictions and then have personally experienced the miraculous, daily power of God to change our desires, our habits, and our futures can tell people who are yet shackled by sin that Jesus is able to radically change the human heart.

Third, it is only on this earth that we have the privilege of calling upon a compassionate Father-God in prayer and watching Him answer those prayers in a way that is "immeasurably more than all we ask or imagine" (Eph 3:20). Admitting our inability to provide for our own needs, illustrating dependency upon a God we can neither see nor touch, and living a life of quiet assurance that God will never abandon us are privileges reserved for our time on this earth. We will not be witnessing to the unbeliever about the goodness of God's provision when we get to heaven. There will be no unbelievers there.

Rather than lamenting the loss of Eden and the distance of heaven, we should rejoice in the unique privileges this world offers, even with all its problems. One more time, let's turn to God's Word for an illustration of this principle.

In 1 Samuel, chapters 1 and 2, we find the heartrending story of Hannah. Often used as an example of miraculous answered prayer, I also see Hannah as a mentor for those of us who need to learn how to stay faithful and true in the midst of life's greatest trials. For those less familiar with the story, here's a thumbnail sketch. Hannah lived in a time in history when a woman's worth was primarily measured by the number of children she could provide for her husband. Hannah's husband, Elkanah, was a religious and loving man who also had a second wife, Peninnah. The entire household was in a sad state of affairs. Hannah was deeply hurt over the fact that she had not been able to get pregnant. Intensifying the disappointment was the ridicule she got at every turn from Peninnah, who had provided several offspring for Elkanah. Peninnah was jealous of the greater love Elkanah showed toward barren Hannah and used every opportunity to make life miserable for Hannah. Elkanah was torn between the two women. He loved his children, and, of course, their mother. But he didn't hide his preference for Hannah, and couldn't understand why his love didn't satisfy her emotional needs.

God's law required Elkanah and his household to travel from their home in Ramathaim to the tabernacle three times each year to worship and sacrifice to the Lord. Elkanah was faithful to God's instruction and made the trips at the appointed times with the appropriate sacrifices, both wives, and all the children Peninnah had borne. These trips were no fun for Hannah. No other occasion throughout the year so poignantly illustrated her barrenness as when Elkanah would distribute the portions of the sacrifice. Peninnah would receive not only her portion, but some for each of the children. And although Elkanah would give Hannah a double portion for herself because of her barrenness, it didn't lessen her grief. As the sacrifices were doled out, Peninnah would smirk and make snide remarks to Hannah. Year after year Hannah was desperately tormented and reduced to tears, her pain so great she couldn't eat. Elkanah continually tried to bring comfort, but it wasn't enough to soothe this woman's heartbreak.

One year, during the time of sacrifice, Hannah got an idea. Suddenly she realized that she could call upon the Lord God to whom sacrifices were being made, the same God who had "closed her womb" and who knew the hearts of all people. After dinner she went to the tabernacle by herself and began to pour out her bitter anguish to the Lord Almighty. This was no small matter to Hannah, and the cries of her heart, mingled with her tears, indicated the intensity of her prayer. "If you will only look upon your servant's misery and remember me, and not forget your servant but give her a son, then I will give him to the Lord for all the days of his life ..." (1 Sm 1:11).

Hannah was finally going to the source of her fulfillment. Neither in the love of Elkanah nor in her own physical abilities could she find the right formula to create a child. But in her Lord there was both compassion for her desperate need and sufficient provision to bring about a miraculous answer. She had come to the right place, with the right request, for the right reason.

Yet the integrity of her heart and the correctness of her action did not prompt a compassionate response from the current priest, Eli. His own life of passivity, gluttony, and self-indulgence tainted every aspect of his ministry. He thought Hannah was drunk (was he looking at himself, maybe?) and rebuked her for her overt display of emotion.

"Oh no, Sir! I'm not drunk! But I am very sad, and I was pouring out my heart to the Lord. Please don't think I'm a wicked woman! For I have been praying out of great anguish and sorrow."

"In that case," Eli said, "cheer up! May the God of Israel grant the request you have asked of Him."

That was all Hannah needed. It was a done deal as far as she was concerned. God may have used a questionable mouthpiece, but devout Hannah recognized truth when she heard it. For the first time in years, Hannah had peace of heart. She had assurance that God was going to turn her sorrow into joy. Suddenly her appetite was back, and she headed for Elkanah's tent to find some food.

It wasn't long after returning home that Hannah became pregnant, and in due time she gave birth to a precious little boy-child, Samuel. I'm certain there was great rejoicing between Elkanah and Hannah. (I'm not so sure about Peninnah.)

The time came around again for the annual trip to the tabernacle. Hannah was beginning to realize the enormous significance of the promise she'd made to God regarding this infant in her arms. Her request of God had been only for this one child, and at this point she had no idea if she would ever bear more children. Could she now give back to God that beloved offspring, as she had promised? Going to the tabernacle with Samuel would only intensify the reality of the eventual separation. When he was weaned, she thought, then she would make the trip and deliver Samuel to Eli to serve the Lord for the rest of his life. Meanwhile, she wanted to stay home. She treasured every moment of time that was hers to be alone with her boy.

"Whatever you think is best," Elkanah agreed. "Stay here for now, and may the Lord help you keep your promise."

So Hannah remained at home while Peninnah and Elkanah made the journey to Jerusalem. Note that as Hannah acted out of a heart of integrity and transparency she did not appear to mask the difficulty of her position. When Elkanah hoped aloud that his wife would be given divine strength to keep her promise, the statement must have come out of his heart of compassion for the woman he loved, a woman who he knew had a very difficult task ahead of her.

I'm sure there were times in the early days of Samuel's life that Hannah questioned her vow to God. Surely a loving, compassionate Father wouldn't require a loving mother to give away her son, her only son. Perhaps God could somehow modify the requirement. Maybe Hannah could keep Samuel at home and train him up "in the fear and admonition of the Lord." She could teach him valuable lessons about a compassionate God who hears and answers prayer, who gives strength to the weary and provides for those unable to provide for themselves. Elkanah was surely a godly husband, and Samuel would greatly benefit from exposure to his leadership in their home. Samuel could learn important social skills as he played with the older half-siblings.

I cannot imagine the tension in Hannah's heart. While eternally thankful to God for the child, she lived with the constant awareness that Samuel was on loan, not given to her and her husband, and that in a very unique way, Samuel belonged completely to God.

Eventually Samuel was weaned and the separation could be delayed no longer. At the appointed time for sacrifices, the enlarged family journeyed to Jerusalem. Walking right up to Eli, Hannah asked, "Sir, do you remember me? I am the woman who stood here several years ago praying to the Lord. I asked the Lord to give me this child, and He has given me my request. Now I am giving him to the Lord, and he will belong to the Lord his whole life."

What immediately follows that statement is one of the most glorious prayers of worship, thanksgiving, and personal victory in all of the Bible. Hannah is overcome with emotion at the privilege of presenting her firstborn child to God. She rejoices, not in the pain of the separation, but in the Lord who has listened to the cry of her heart and provided miraculous life to a barren woman.

"Then Hannah prayed and said:
    'My heart rejoices in the Lord;
in the Lord my horn is lifted high.
My mouth boasts over my enemies,
for I delight in your deliverance.

    'There is no one holy like the Lord;
there is no one besides you;
there is no Rock like our God.

    'Do not keep talking so proudly
or let your mouth speak such arrogance,
for the Lord is a God who knows,
and by him deeds are weighed.

    'The bows of the warriors are broken,
but those who stumbled are armed with strength.
Those who were full hire themselves out for food,
but those who were hungry hunger no more.
She who was barren has borne seven children,
but she who has had many sons pines away.

    'The Lord brings death and makes alive;
he brings down to the grave and raises up.
The Lord sends poverty and wealth;
he humbles and he exalts.

    He raises the poor from the dust
and lifts the needy from the ash heap;
he seats them with princes

and has them inherit a throne of honor.

'For the foundations of the earth are the Lord's;
upon them he has set the world.
He will guard the feet of his saints,
but the wicked will be silenced in darkness.

'It is not by strength that one prevails;
those who oppose the Lord will be shattered.
He will thunder against them from heaven;
the Lord will judge the ends of the earth.

'He will give strength to his king
and exalt the horn of his anointed.'"

1 SAMUEL 2:1-10

The next verse says, "Then Elkanah went home to Ramah, but the boy ministered before the Lord."

Ouch. Some might have you believe that Hannah never grieved the absence of Samuel from her daily life. I don't believe that for a minute! If you believe that doing the right thing won't ever result in pain, discomfort, financial struggles, or relational challenges, then you have your head in some pseudobiblical belief ... and it may literally drive you crazy if you keep thinking that way. Jesus did the right thing and He was murdered. Paul did the right thing and was put to death for his faith. John did the right thing and was banished to a desert island. Most of the Psalms were written in the midst of difficulty. Most of the epistles were written in prison. John Bunyan wrote *Pilgrims Progress* in jail. And if you think that all of this is ancient history, let me remind you that more

Christians have been martyred for their faith during this century than in all previous centuries combined! In 1995 alone, carefully documented reports tell us that 165,000 Christians were put to death for their unwavering stand for the Lord Jesus. Even as I write these words, Christians in Pakistan are being tortured and put to death, some by crucifixion. All for being people of integrity.

The High Price of Integrity

During our lifetimes here we have in us a marvelous mixture of both well-being and woe. The wonderful risen Christ resides in us, certainly, but so do we experience the wretchedness and pain of the fall of Adam. Our lives are a tapestry of living and dying. I don't expect to face crucifixion of my body today, but I may find my reputation or my pride hanging on a cross someone prepares for me.

Recently I gave my testimony at an event where several hundred women were present. Following the presentation it seemed the applause would never stop, and I reveled in the goodness of God to allow these women to hear my heart as I encouraged them toward a Christlike lifestyle of openness and transparency. But not everyone was positive about what I had said. Two women stood in line for a considerable time in order to speak to me face to face. As the enemy of my soul would have it, they were the last ones to shake my hand and talk with me, so, naturally, they are the ones I remember. Their mission was clear: I had to be rebuked for certain "advice" I had given which was dangerous, unchristian, and unhealthy for believers. At that point I was so physically and emotionally weary that I couldn't come up with an appropriate, in-your-face response, so I just stood there and tried to be as gracious as possible.

Now, I'm not implying that I don't require accountability for what I say and do. Just like everybody else, I can be far too simplistic in my advice, too prideful in my presentations, and can fail to address each and every variation on whatever theme I'm covering each day. For those who truly desire to bring balance and wisdom to my awareness, I am grateful. I only wish they would take the time to pray for a couple of days and then write me a long letter explaining their position. You may be certain I would remember their advice better and be more prone to accept their admonitions!

As my friend and I were driving home following the event, I told her what had happened. "Miriam," she said tenderly, "that is part of the price you pay for being so honest and open about your own struggles. If you were teaching from a book somebody else had written, then these women who disagree would have to take up their arguments with the author, not with you. But since you are called to share from the pain of your own life, you have to be prepared to deal directly with those who question your motives or your methods."

She was right. I was reminded of the words I had prayed as we drove to the luncheon: "Lord, I give up control of this day. Please do in my heart, and in the hearts of the listeners, exactly what You want, even though it might not be what I have planned." I had meant that prayer from the bottom of my heart. What I didn't know, of course, was the level of discomfort and disappointment, as well as joy, that the answer to that prayer would bring. Still, the lesson was clear: As God grants me the courage to be real, I must give Him the glory for the applause I get in response, as well as the opportunity to help me deal with the criticism.

F.B. Meyer says, "It is thus that human life is made up: Brightness and gloom; shadow and sun; long tracks of cloud, succeeded by brilliant glints of light."* One of the most needless frustrations we will ever experience is that of attempting to turn our present environment into a replica of God's original creation, Eden. Get a grip: it just ain't gonna happen (forgive me, English majors)! But what is just as glorious is the thrill of watching God invade this imperfect life with His perfection. To wait until things (finances, personalities, relationships, weight, problems of every sort) change is to unnecessarily delay God's blessing upon those very issues.

Jesus said, "I've told you all this so that trusting me, you will be unshakable and assured, deeply at peace. In this godless world you will continue to experience difficulties. But take heart! I've conquered the world" (Jn 16:33, THE MESSAGE). His provision, protection, and promise for our "east of Eden" todays will sustain us as we wait expectantly for our glorious tomorrows.

*F.B. Meyer, *Abraham* (Fort Washington, Penn.: Christian Literature Crusader, 1993), 79-80.

True Reflections

1. This chapter begins with the story of the rediscovered ring and the resultant test of my integrity. Can you identify some issue that is causing your integrity to be put to the test? Are you willing to ask God to help you do the right thing, right now?

2. Are you spending too much of your time and energy attempting to make yourself, your church, your environment, or your world into a perfect place? How could that same time and energy be better invested?

3. Can you remember the several ways in which this life is unique, different from Eden or heaven? Can you think of other blessings this world offers which heaven cannot give?

4. Hannah spent many years living with both the negative (loneliness) and positive (clear conscience) results of her decision to be a woman of integrity. Are you willing to be such a woman, no matter the consequences?

The Velveteen Christian

In Margery Williams's magnificent children's classic, *The Velveteen Rabbit*, an imaginary conversation between simple toys reveals the complex, beautiful truth about what is involved in living with integrity and transparency. The Rabbit articulates in bottom-line fashion the same question this book has been posing from the first page to the last: "What is *real?*"

"'Real isn't how you are made,' answered the Skin Horse. 'It's a thing that happens to you. When a child loves you for a long, long time, not just to play with, but *really* loves you, then you become Real.'"

The Rabbit then goes on to ask if pain is part of the process, and if becoming Real happens, "'all at once, like being wound up … or bit by bit?'"

The very wise Skin Horse doesn't deny the reality of how bad the hurt may be in becoming real, or that the process generally takes a long time. He has learned that truth is essential to

165

any transparent relationship. The Skin Horse goes on to warn: "'That's why [becoming real] doesn't often happen to people who break easily, or have sharp edges, or who have to be carefully kept. Generally, by the time you are Real, most of your hair has been loved off, and your eyes drop out and you get loose in the joints and very shabby. But these things don't matter at all, because once you are Real you can't be ugly, except to people who don't understand.'"

As women who are *really* loved by God and who desire to be courageously authentic, I propose that we learn to proudly label ourselves Velveteen Christians. We are women whom God holds close as we are rubbed to shabbiness by sandpaper people. We are women whose joints are continually being loosened by the shaking of disappointments, failures, and ongoing struggles. But we are women who, as a result of the painful, usually extended process, are being transformed by the love and power of the Holy Spirit into people who are not ashamed of who we are, with all our foibles, and who are not afraid to expose our current challenges, as well as our victories.

There will always be "people who don't understand," who will be quick to ridicule our shabbiness and criticize our convictions. In our resolve to be women who are real in a world of duplicity and falseness, the choice to stand by our convictions and confess them publicly will provide both the best and worst experiences we can imagine. Being true to our convictions does not insulate us from the attacks of those who would disagree. In fact, sometimes I think people of integrity just frustrate others to death. One person's conviction of heart often causes others discomfort, and the only way they know how to save face is to ridicule the one who stands confident in who she is and what she believes.

And yet, the world is longing for women of godly discernment: thinking, praying, contemplating, knowledgeable women who know *why* they believe what they say they believe. Women who, when faced with issues about which they are truly uninformed, are confident enough to shut up, knowing that shutting up isn't the same as giving in. Women who are willing to pay a personal price to be true to themselves.

To Thine Own Self Be True

As we examine our hearts and minds in an attempt to increase our integrity and courage, we need only look to Jesus. He neither pacified the sinner, nor ignored the cries of the sincere. He never falsified a claim about Himself, nor did He deny the amazing truth of who He really was. He never once thought He was popular because He was bright, cute, or wealthy. He fully faced the reality that most people crowded around Him because He healed the sick, raised the dead, and provided lunch. Jesus never led His followers to believe the lie that life would be easy. Rather, He exemplified for every one of us the real danger of living with eternal values in mind. Jesus' whole life was the ultimate example of what being real is all about: be true to who you are, no matter where you are, no matter the expectations of others, and even when it's dangerous.

Consider two women in the Bible who exemplify much of what this book is attempting to teach: how to become a woman of confidence, of strength of character, of integrity, of courage. The first is Queen Esther. Here is a woman who not only had startling physical beauty, but also was politically savvy, was intuitive about men, and knew how to oversee a kingdom-size kitchen. Added to that were significant wisdom and integrity. It was these character traits that enabled her to be a woman of strength and confidence.

Let me recap the story for you. About 475 years before the birth of Christ there was a very powerful world figure called Xerxes, the fifth king of Persia. He ruled over 127 provinces from India to Ethiopia. According to Charles Swindoll, in his book *Esther: A Woman of Strength and Dignity,* "Archaeologists excavating at Susa have unearthed inscriptions in which this king refers to himself as, 'The great king. The king of kings. The king of the lands occupied by many races. The king of this great earth.'" Old Xerxes didn't struggle with an inferiority complex!

We catch up with this character about the time he was throwing a major gala for all the political leaders of the neighboring countries. His motivation was to win their allegiance against the rest of the known world, and against Greece in particular. This party was bigger than Christmas Eve, Independence Day, the first daughter's wedding, and the Super Bowl all rolled into one. For six months the male representatives from all of these countries had reveled in all the good wine and fabulous food they could consume.

Meanwhile, the current Queen Vashti, who was a real looker herself, had her hands full entertaining the wives and concubines of these men at another tent on the palace grounds. They hadn't been invited to party with the guys.

Just before the king was about to send the guests back home, he threw one more giant feast, seven days and nights of revelry. Eventually all the drinking and gluttony got to him, and he was "in high spirits from wine" (Est 1:10). He decided to produce the pièce de résistance, his gorgeous queen, and put her on display for all his guests. When his attendants went to summon Queen Vashti, however, she refused to come. The humiliated king became furious at her insubordination and banished her from his presence forever. Her punishment was to serve as a lesson to all wives who might be thinking of having their own minds: do what your husband asks, or else!

The guests went home, and now Vashti was gone, too. The palace became a silent, lonely place for the aging king. His worried advisors attempted to encourage him by quickly initiating the process of finding Vashti's replacement.

Enter Esther stage right. Chosen from a long parade of striking beauties, the young orphan girl became Xerxes' new queen. If the Biblical narrative had ended at this point, we could have settled down into our easy chairs and thought, "What a lovely thing to happen to Esther. Reminds me of Cinderella. Poor girl makes good." That would have been nice, but not complete, because the real saga only begins at this point. I have chosen so far not to reveal one essential point: Esther was not Persian. She was a Jew, raised by her cousin

Mordecai in this foreign country. And just as I failed to tell you that fact, so Esther also chose not to inform her husband of her heritage.

In every good suspense story there has to be a villain. Ours is named Haman—a downright dastardly fellow, evil, impressed with himself, and driven by an insatiable appetite for climbing the political ladder. King Xerxes had honored him as the highest nobleman in the land, but Mordecai had refused to kiss up to Haman the way everyone else did. Haman hated Mordecai and wanted him dead. In order to pull this off without tipping his hand to the king, he convinced the unsuspecting Xerxes that the Jews who resided in Persia at the time were a menace to the kingdom and ought to be summarily destroyed. The king allowed Haman to unduly influence him, gave into the idea, and signed a decree that all Jews were to be exterminated, no questions asked!

Queen Esther was not required to co-sign the decree, and thus had no clue about what Haman and her hubby had just done. The word was out on the streets, however, and Cousin Mordecai was fully aware of the imminent danger. He sent word to Esther that not only were all Jews in a very precarious position, but her own heritage would most certainly be discovered and she would soon join Vashti at the home for "Queens No Longer!"

Although the outer beauty of Queen Esther had been obvious all along, it was at this point that her inner beauty, integrity, and courage began to emerge. She knew she must do something to save her people ... and herself.

She started by stopping. She called upon her support group, including Mordecai and all his Jewish acquaintances, and told them to join her in a specific period of fasting and prayer. Out of these three days of isolation and focus came a plan of action, but far more than that, the courage to carry out the plan. I'm sure Esther was fully aware that the reason her predecessor was no longer in the palace was because she hadn't shown up when she was supposed to. Now here was Esther, about to show up where she wasn't invited—an action which was not only against the law, but was subject to a punishment of death, unless the king was in a particularly good mood on the day in question.

Esther's courage and conviction couldn't have been articulated more clearly: "If I perish, I perish" (Est 4:16). When Esther walked in on the king uninvited, the significance of the moment could not be exaggerated. The existence of an entire race of people came down to the moment the door unexpectedly opened and Esther stood, vulnerable and alone, before the king.

This moment reminds me of the story of Elisha and his nervous servant in 2 Kings 6:14-18: One night the king of Syria sent a great army with many chariots and horses to surround the city. When the prophet's servant got up early the next morning and went outside, there were troops, horses, and chariots everywhere. "Oh, my lord, my master, what shall we do?" he cried out to Elisha. "Don't be afraid!" Elisha told him. "Those who are with us are more than those who are with them." Then Elisha prayed, "Lord, open his eyes so he may see!" And the Lord opened the young man's eyes so that he could see horses of fire and chariots of fire everywhere upon the mountain! As the Syrian army advanced upon them, Elisha prayed, "Lord, please make them blind." And He did.

I would imagine that if we could have had the same kind of "opened eyes" to see into the king's throne room that day, we would have seen hosts of angels going before that nervous young girl, preparing the heart of her royal husband, surrounding her with safety, and providing courage beyond her human capacities. It seems to be the nature of such events: When we are put in circumstances over which we have very little control, but where we are called upon to stand for the right, God has a way of stepping in, preparing the way, and bringing about the desired results. "I will go before thee, and make the crooked places straight; I will break in pieces the gates of brass, and cut in sunder the bars of iron" (Is 45:2, KJV).

My personal conviction is that everything else that went on after this pivotal moment in the throne room was anticlimactic. Sure, there were the banquets which Esther prepared for Haman and the king, and the unexpected promotion of Cousin Mordecai to a place of honor, the amending of the decree ordering the deaths of the Jews, and eventually the impaling and hanging of Haman on the seven-story-high gallows which he had prepared for Mordecai. But all of that happened as a result of Esther's courage to be true to herself and her people.

I don't suppose that anyone who is at this moment reading these words has the fate of an entire nation resting on their shoulders, as Queen Esther did. But I do believe that many of us face decisions that may well alter not only our own futures, but also those of the people we influence. Our "people" aren't a whole nation, but our family, our employer, our church congregation, our friends—all who will ultimately benefit or suffer as a result of the choices we make.

What determines the choices you are making these days? Long ago I learned that peer pressure does not end when the teenage years have passed. The longing to be included, to be respected, to be needed stays with us until we die. It's a good thing it does, or we'd all become curmudgeons! But when our desire to be accepted overpowers our courage to stand by our convictions, then we've traded integrity for popularity. Some of us mistakenly measure our spirituality by our popularity with other Christians, as if we believe they cast the all-important vote. But being a real woman means giving up following respectable people to follow God. If we are to be women of integrity, we must be ready to say what we believe to be true and what actions we are prepared to take based upon those beliefs, no matter what the consequences.

Probably no other woman in Scripture so profoundly exhibited personal strength in the face of possible public humiliation or even death as Queen Esther. Yet, reading the story from this perspective, we have discovered that she was no more alone in her moment of destiny than you or I are alone as we face critical choices today. Our courage to be real grows out of the conviction that the ultimate place of safety is in the strong arms of our Savior: "He tends his flock like a shepherd: He gathers the lambs in his arms and carries them close to his heart" (Is 40:11).

Devoted and True

Let's look at another model of confidence, integrity, and courage. The contrasts are startling while the lessons remain consistent. We found Esther in an opulent palace, no doubt spending some of her time on a high throne, looking down at the people. In John 12:1-8 we find another courageous woman: Mary of Bethany, in a simple home, sitting on the floor, looking up into the eyes of Jesus. This is the much-esteemed quiet Mary, sister of Lazarus, whom Jesus had recently raised from the dead, and of Martha (could her last name have been Stewart?), the ever-busy one with whom so many of us identify.

Each person mentioned in this short story was well acquainted with death. The story of the death and miraculous resurrection of Lazarus was fresh in the minds of this family, and of the disciples of Jesus, who watched it happen. And now here sat Lazarus, fellowshipping at the dinner table with Jesus, who Himself would die in less than a week.

As sensitive, intuitive Mary listened to Jesus talk, she suddenly grasped the truth that seemed to pass right over the heads of everyone else in the room that night: Jesus really was going to die, and soon. Mary's heart began to pound in her chest. The deep affection and adoration she felt for Jesus drove her to her feet and down the hall to her bedroom. In a place reserved for private treasures, Mary carefully uncovered her most precious possession: a sealed alabaster box filled with spikenard, an ointment used to anoint the dead. She had paid an extravagant price for this one-pound box, about a year's wages. It had probably been purchased to be used at the time of her own death.

Clutching the treasure close to her heart, Mary returned to the crowded room and sat down again in front of Jesus. Hesitating just long enough to look once more into His face, without a word she broke open the box, and the ointment spilled over His feet. The remarkable scent drowned the conversation and the appetites of those gathered around the table.

Immediately Mary was the focus of attention as she took down her long hair and began to wipe Jesus' feet. Open, silent mouths and stern frowns revealed the disbelief taking shape in the hearts and minds of the disciples. Why would Mary do such a foolish, extravagant thing? As she wiped the ointment, now mixed with her own tears, from Jesus' feet, all heaven stopped and bowed in honor of the lone woman in her courageous act of love for her Lord.

"Jesus!" The strident voice of Judas shattered the sacred moment. "Why are you letting her do that? What a waste! We could have used that money to feed the homeless."

Now all eyes turned to Jesus. Clearly the life of Judas had proven he cared nothing for the poor, but that did not negate the fact that, in effect, a great deal of money had just been poured out on the floor. Mary continued to wipe Jesus' feet, but now a knowing, peaceful smile replaced the trembling of her lips. The murmurs of the disciples, the accusation of Judas, even the stare of Martha, who almost missed the whole event while she bustled in the kitchen—none of these mattered to Mary. Settled in the confidence that Jesus fully understood her motives and actions, Mary ignored the judgment and open criticism of those around her. The love of Jesus for Mary produced every ounce of strength and courage she needed in the face of unwarranted, but very real, ridicule.

Jesus stopped long enough to gain His composure, wiped His own eyes, and responded directly to Judas, and indirectly to all of us. His tone of voice was as tender as Judas' had been piercing.

"Oh, come on now, Judas. You know and I know that the needs of the poor of this world have absolutely nothing to do with what just went on here. What Mary has done is to understand what none of the rest of you has. I am about to die. What she just did was in response to the deep sorrow of her heart and her love for Me. Leave her alone."

The disciples realized that, one more time, they'd missed the point, failed to seize the moment, and disappointed the Master.

Mary's act of devotion revealed her true self. She did not act out of character with the person she had always been: a woman unwilling to be pressured by family, tradition, or public opinion, a woman who would quietly revolt against the expectations of her stronger sister in order to fulfill her own call. Mary would be the woman God wanted her to be, no matter what anyone said.

The Joy of Living Real

In my own life, God's grace continues daily to supply sufficient courage that helps me to be real in all my encounters. Most of my hair is loved off, my rigid joints are broken loose, my eyes are cried out, and my soul is shabby—but I am joyful.

What about you? Have you discovered that beyond the brokenness involved in the process of becoming real is an awesome freedom and joy to be exactly who God created you to be? No longer do you have anything to hide. Living with integrity grants you a steady supply of God's grace, which gives you the courage to be real and stand up for what you believe, no matter what the cost. As a woman who is deeply loved and totally secure, you can risk everything in order to be a woman of conviction and to point others toward Jesus.

As you contemplate the next steps on your journey toward confidence, integrity, and transparency, let me encourage you with one more story.

It is Christmas Eve. A seven-year-old girl cries quietly as she gets ready for bed. This has to have been the longest day of her short life. There is no bustling about in the kitchen, making preparations for Christmas dinner. The refrigerator is empty. There are no last-minute tree-trimming sessions. There is no Christmas tree this year. There is no secret gift-wrapping by her mommy and daddy. There is no money for presents.

As the little girl tries bravely to smile on her way to bed, her daddy senses her sorrow and comes to tuck her in and comfort her heart.

"My precious little one," he says, "I don't know how God is going to do it, but you can bet everything is going to be all right, because Jesus is real, and He has promised never to fail us. Somehow, tomorrow morning, we're going to have Christmas—you just wait and see."

Though the tears of unknowing still fall, the little girl trusts the daddy she can see, and even at that tender age is learning to trust the heavenly Father she can't see. Eventually she falls asleep.

The daddy goes into the living room and kneels down beside the big rocking chair. "Oh, God, You who came in reality to our earth so long ago, please hear this prayer of a father's heart. I cannot hide from You my deep disappointment that there isn't provision for the family You gave me. You know the truth of my soul: I long to give so much to them, and yet, so far, there doesn't seem to be any hope of the kind of Christmas they long for. It's Christmas Eve, Lord God. Somehow, some way, please, for the sake of the children who are asleep, please provide what You think is best. Amen."

Sometime later the little girl is stirred by noises. In a sleepy stupor she peeks through the crack in her bedroom door and sees the small living room electric with activity. People—happy people—are everywhere. So are bags of food, colorfully wrapped presents, and, miracle of miracles, a Christmas tree, decorated with tinsel and lights and an angel on top!

Believing she must be dreaming, and afraid the wonder will go away if she really wakes up, she goes back to bed and falls soundly asleep.

"Sweetheart, get up! It's Christmas morning!" Her daddy's voice is filled with joy. "Come and see what God brought in the night!"

Barely remembering the events of the night before, she stumbles into the living room, where her mommy and brother are already waiting. Right there, in front of her eyes, is a real Christmas tree, with lights, tinsel, and an angel on top! She can smell the real turkey that's already roasting in the oven.

And then her wide-eyed gaze settles on a doll buggy with a beautiful doll inside, the very first toy this little girl has ever had. She dances around the tree, holding the doll and singing, "Joy to the world, the Lord *has* come!"

This Christmas miracle was my first personal encounter with the power, provision, and overwhelming love of a *real*, almighty, compassionate God. A God who would prompt kind folk from a mission church sixty miles away to sacrifice their own Christmas Eve festivities in order to bring Christmas to a poor preacher and his family.

I know that life is complicated. I know there are rarely any simple solutions. I know that becoming real, transparent, and confident can be a long, difficult, and tedious struggle. But I also know we serve a *real* God. A God who hears the *real* cries of our hearts. A God who understands the *real* dreams of our souls. A God who asks only that we be real with Him and with each other.

May our real God make us real women.

True Reflections

1. Is it difficult for you to stand by your convictions in the face of those who disagree? In such situations, do you find yourself becoming more assertive and defensive, or quieter and injured? Which aspects of your character does God need to adjust in order to make you a discerning, confident, knowledgeable woman?

2. Do you identify most with the public persona of Queen Esther, or with the private Mary of Bethany? Are you giving God permission to use your unique strengths to manifest the courage and integrity He can supply?

Miriam Conrad welcomes your inquiries
regarding speaking engagements.
She can be contacted at
P.O. Box 461288, Escondido, CA 92046-1288.
E-mail address: transparency@juno.com